The Craft of
Writing the Novel

BOOKS BY PHYLLIS REYNOLDS NAYLOR

For Adults

CRAZY LOVE: AN AUTOBIOGRAPHI-
  CAL ACCOUNT OF MARRIAGE AND
  MADNESS
REVELATIONS

IN SMALL DOSES
UNEXPECTED PLEASURES
THE CRAFT OF WRITING THE NOVEL

For Young Adults

GRASSHOPPERS IN THE SOUP
KNEE DEEP IN ICE CREAM
TO SHAKE A SHADOW
WHEN RIVERS MEET
DARK SIDE OF THE MOON
THE PRIVATE I
MAKING IT HAPPEN
SHIPS IN THE NIGHT
NO EASY CIRCLE
HOW TO FIND YOUR WONDERFUL
  SOMEONE
AN AMISH FAMILY
WALKING THROUGH THE DARK

A CHANGE IN THE WIND
SHADOWS ON THE WALL
FACES IN THE WATER
FOOTPRINTS AT THE WINDOW
A STRING OF CHANCES
NEVER BORN A HERO
THE SOLOMON SYSTEM
A TRIANGLE HAS FOUR SIDES
NIGHT CRY
THE DARK OF THE TUNNEL
THE KEEPER
THE YEAR OF THE GOPHER
SEND NO BLESSINGS

For Children

THE GALLOPING GOAT AND OTHER
  STORIES
WHAT THE GULLS WERE SINGING
JENNIFER JEAN, CROSS-EYED
  QUEEN
THE NEW SCHOOLMASTER
A NEW YEAR'S SURPRISE
MEET MURDOCK
TO MAKE A WEE MOON
WRESTLE THE MOUNTAIN
TO WALK THE SKY PATH
WITCH'S SISTER
GETTING ALONG IN YOUR FAMILY
WITCH WATER
THE WITCH HERSELF
HOW I CAME TO BE A WRITER
GETTING ALONG WITH YOUR
  FRIENDS
HOW LAZY CAN YOU GET?
EDDIE, INCORPORATED
GETTING ALONG WITH YOUR
  TEACHERS

ALL BECAUSE I'M OLDER
THE BOY WITH THE HELIUM HEAD
THE MAD GASSER OF BESSLEDORF
  STREET
OLD SADIE AND THE CHRISTMAS
  BEAR
THE AGONY OF ALICE
THE BODIES IN THE BESSLEDORF
  HOTEL
THE BABY, THE BED, AND THE
  ROSE
BEETLES, LIGHTLY TOASTED
MAUDIE IN THE MIDDLE
ONE OF THE THIRD GRADE
  THONKERS
ALICE IN RAPTURE, SORT OF
KEEPING A CHRISTMAS SECRET
BERNIE AND THE BESSLEDORF
  GHOST
KING OF THE PLAYGROUND
SHILOH

The Craft
of Writing
the Novel

by Phyllis Reynolds Naylor

Publishers   THE WRITER, INC.   Boston

Library of Congress Cataloging-in-Publication Data

Naylor, Phyllis Reynolds.
  The craft of writing the novel / by Phyllis Reynolds Naylor.
    p.   cm.
  ISBN 0-87116-153-2 :
  1. Fiction—Technique. I. Title.
PN3365.N39   1989   88-32415
808.3—dc19   CIP

Printed in the United States of America

To all the editors, past and present, whose letters of acceptance and rejection have taught me whatever I know about writing; and to my husband, Rex, whose unsparing criticism of each of my manuscripts has lightened the workload of these editors considerably.

CONTENTS

The Craft of
Writing the Novel

🎜 1

The Spark

GEORGE ORWELL IS SUPPOSED to have said that he wrote so that his fifth-grade teacher might see his work and be sorry that she had misjudged him.

Whatever it is that makes us write—a drive, an addiction, a compulsion—we write because we must, and can only hope that when we've finished, we will have accomplished what we set out to do, and that our work will be published. If published, we hope it will be read, and if read, we hope most of all that it will be remembered.

This book is not an instruction manual or recipe book, for in art there are no guarantees that if we follow steps one through ten, the work will not be stillborn. What gives a manuscript life is the most difficult of all to prescribe; a writer goes about his craft with an eye on technique and an ear to his heart. What we bring of ourselves to our writing is something that we alone can give. But we can always improve on the way we use our material, hone our sentences, and perfect our style. There is never an end to this learning.

The "right" idea

In the beginning, of course, is the idea. Sometimes it comes to us in full bloom, and sometimes it is only a seed, a germ of an idea so intangible we cannot seem to take hold right away. When writers are asked where they get their ideas, they often pause, knowing that the answer expected is "From the newspaper," or "Memories of my childhood," or "Based on my time in the Navy." The truth may be that they aren't quite sure themselves. Usually, a novel is made up of "something old, something new, something borrowed, something blue"—a patchwork of ideas stitched patiently together.

Some ideas develop so gradually over a period of months or even years that a writer has visions of his novel being published posthumously. The parts fall slowly into place like the pieces of a puzzle, and at long last he thinks, looking at the notes before him, "Perhaps I've got a book here." At other times, he may get up in the morning and in the minute or two it takes him to brush his teeth, an idea strikes like a thunderbolt and he says, "My god, this is it!" He hasn't even put the cap back on the toothpaste.

On the front page of every newspaper there are numerous ideas for novels. We are bombarded with stimuli from many directions—conversations we overhear in restaurants, the gossip of neighbors, arguments on a bus. . . . A well-meaning friend may phone with an idea for a book "you just have to write!" What makes one idea so different from another, to be selected from all the rest? Why is this one chosen over that one, to be carefully tended, nurtured, and turned at last into a novel?

It sounds mystical to say that, with practice, you'll "know" when an idea is right, just as a person "knows" he is in love. You may in the end be all wrong, of course, and wish you had never thought of it, but there is a certain madness that grabs at you and doesn't let go—a leap in the chest, a catch in the throat—as though someone has revved up your motor, and you can't shut it off.

The attraction may come on swiftly or slowly, but for an idea to become the spark that will ignite the writing of a novel, there are usually two emotions involved: a rush of enthusiasm and a feeling of specialness about the story. What makes it special is your conviction that you have something unique to contribute, something of yourself to give.

A friend's idea for a suspense novel about smuggling, set in Mexico and based on a conversation he overheard on a plane, may indeed, be an excellent idea—for someone else. If you know very little about the drug trade and have never been to Mexico, the book should probably be left for another author. If however, in spite of its drawbacks, the idea connects with something inside of you—a subplot, a personality, a mood that would work itself perfectly into such a setting—you may find yourself enthusiastic enough to do all the necessary research. In such a case, you attach your friend's idea to something you already know or feel or are. We all see the world differently according to our personalities and experiences; consequently the same subject given to thirty different authors will produce thirty different books, each unique.

Developing an idea
It is difficult to say just when the idea for my novel *Unexpected Pleasures* began. I remember rolling over one night and, in my half sleep, being acutely conscious of the motions of my body. Like a cat stretching, I felt my legs uncoil, my toes extend, and I thought "I am so conscious of this moment that I could describe it in detail in a book."

Ideas arriving in the middle of the night are sometimes akin to hallucinations, but this time the idea, trivial as it seemed, stayed with me the following morning, and I decided that I would probably use it in a book for teen-agers, in a scene where a girl crawls into bed beside her sister. In my mind's eye, I placed them on a sofa bed in a house trailer. Immediately a line of dialogue whispered in my ear: "Thomasine, put-that-down-I'm-gonna-hitcha." There was no picture accompanying this line. I knew that at some point in the book one girl would say it to the other, but I did not know how it would work itself into the plot—I didn't even *know* the plot. It was with these two random ideas, though, that the book had its start.

I was not in love with it yet, however. As the plot came more into focus, I realized that it was not a novel for teenagers but for adults. The man whom I had originally envisioned as the father in the book would be the young girl's future husband instead—an ironworker, a builder of bridges. That's when I fell in love.

My experience of turning over in bed became the opening paragraphs of the second chapter:

> "When I come back to bed from using the commode, Thomasine was over on my side. She always does that way. Like a cat, seeking out every little bit of warmth. Just once in my life, I thought, I'd like to have me a bed all to myself, but seeing as how I was marrying Foster Williams on Saturday, didn't look like that was about to happen.
>
> " 'Thomasine, get your legs over,' I said. She only purred.
>
> "I rapped her knee hard with my knuckles, and this time she slowly started to unwind herself. She rolled over on her back, stretching her legs full out, toes all pointy, then gives this little grunt and flops over on the other side, drawing her knees up close to her chest."

In this novel, it is not the main character who does the turning, as I had first thought it would be; it is her sister. And while both this scene and the later admonition, "Thomasine, put-that-down-I'm-gonna-hitcha," are in the story, they are by no means the focal point. Sometimes the ideas that start the novel end up taking a back seat in the story; they may even be discarded as scenes come into focus. No matter. What is important is the spark—the excitement about what you have to give to this novel—that will carry you along from one chapter to the next. Your early ideas may serve only as kindling, yet without them the book might never be written.

But where did I fit into this story? What did I bring to it that was uniquely mine? I had never lived in a house trailer, had a husband twice my age, or known a bridge builder. I couldn't even ride a ferris wheel comfortably, much less walk on nine-inch beams of steel 300 feet above the water.

A writer often draws on similar, but not identical, experiences. I certainly knew what it was like to be poor as a child, and to yearn for a room of my own, a bed of my own. And it was my fear of heights that put me in awe of bridge builders, that induced me to collect clippings on ironworkers almost twelve years before I knew how I would use them. So these experiences and feelings worked themselves into my novel.

Some authors begin a book with the idea for a certain character and build the novel from that. Others use a particular situation as a base: the occupation of the protagonist, or a special setting—a time, a city, a mood. . . . It may vary not only from writer to writer but from book to book. Authors debate the issue endlessly. For every example of a successful novel that had its beginning with a character, there will be an example of a much-praised book that began first as a plot. And though writers listen intently to each other and are fascinated with their differences, chances are they rush back home and continue writing in the way that suits them best.

The happy part about idea-hunting is that it comes more easily with experience. The more writers write, the better attuned they will be to possibilities. Beginning writers too often think in terms of a dramatic once-in-a-lifetime situation and overlook drama in the ordinary, hidden potential of the mundane.

Brainstorming

If ideas don't come readily, actively searching them out is something like free-associating in psychotherapy, allowing any thought at all to enter your head without censorship. You can train yourself to do this. In a solitary brainstorming session, jot down all the random story ideas that occur to you, whether or not they have been done before and no matter how much difficulty you may have in researching them. Just let them come, one idea leading to the next and the next. Such a list might read:

Husband discovers that boss is wife's lover.
Minister suspected of child abuse.
The story of grandmother's sofa pillow.
Holding a U.S. senator hostage.
A woman coming to terms with childlessness.
A murder planned to occur at the height of a hurricane.
Someone discovers a dark secret about a friend.
An idealist whose principles are tested on the job.

At this point these are not yet sparks, only ideas, and vague ones at that. You encourage your mind to roam without having to pin down the theme or the intricacies of plot. When the brainstorming is over, put your list away for a day or a week, letting the ideas steep in the back of your mind while you think of other things. At a later time, when you're fresh and relaxed, take the list out again and see what you've got, circling the ones with possibilities. Such a session might go like this:

Boss is wife's lover. Perhaps it doesn't strike any sparks, and you suppose it's been done too many times.

Minister suspected of child abuse. Here you may remember a man in your hometown and the shame of his family when he was arrested for exposing himself in public. You circle this one.

Grandmother's sofa pillow. Wasn't there a story behind this pillow? Didn't she receive it as an engagement present, and wasn't there supposed to be a message embroidered on it somewhere? No book here, you think—maybe a short story, or possibly a scene in a novel.

A senator held hostage. You may decide you don't know enough about the workings of Congress to do a convincing job.

A woman coming to terms with childlessness. A good theme, perhaps, but for someone else.

A murder planned to occur at the height of a hurricane is an idea that may appeal to you, except that you know very little about hurricanes. You might want to research it, though. Circle it.

Someone discovers a dark secret about a friend. You like the dark secret part, though you don't know why. Circle it.

Scratch the *idealist whose principles are tested on the job.* You recall a recent review of a book on the same theme and lose interest.

Out of eight ideas, you may have selected three. You think about them for weeks or months before one of those ideas seems to be growing, developing, taking on appendages, subplots and characters.

Once this happens, excitement begins to build, enthusiasm mounts, and the pot that was simmering on a back burner boils over. The idea that began as a scribbled line on paper—"Minister suspected of child abuse"—becomes the story of a tortured man who has conquered a past problem of child molestation; he has married and started a new life, only to be accused falsely of sexually molesting a teen-age girl.

As an author, you will contribute other parts of yourself as well as your memory of the man in your hometown: something of your own religious background, perhaps; the New England setting in which you were reared; memories of the gossip about your neighbor—the way he was shunned at social gatherings, and how his daughter ran off with the first boy who came along. You may also remember how everyone felt about this girl—pitied her, maybe—but no one made a particular effort to be friendly. As the plot develops, it seems to suck more and more from you—guilt over your own avoidance of this girl, remorse, curiosity, and a sense of justice—until at last the real and the imaginary are blended into a tightly woven fabric, and it is almost impossible to separate the different strands.

It is at this jumping-off point that authors must call upon their art, making the leap from their own experience into imagination. "Journalism is conscientious to the available facts," John Cheever once said. "In fiction one uses the available facts merely to create a mood, an illusion." A novel is not a diary, enlarged and expanded, recording events that actually happened in the writers' lives or to their friends. Rather, it is a combination of the real and the imaginary that eventually becomes something all its own, apart from either parent. And this is where the artistry comes in.

For some writers, experienced authors as well as the novice, an idea is a "sometime thing." There are long barren stretches in which there seem to be no workable ideas at all. More than once, the author considers a second job.

Other writers may have to fend off ideas as if they were bees at a picnic supper. These ideas intrude upon the novels they are working on at the moment, loudly demanding attention, and often receive the same enthusiasm with which a mother of eleven children greets the news that she is pregnant once again.

And there are a few lucky writers who, about halfway through the last draft of their final chapter, suddenly "know" what their next book will be. Not many writers, perhaps, but some.

Most of us will go through these different phases at one time or another. There will be a strangely fallow period for an author who was previously prolific; or for writers who were never swept off their feet before by inspiration, a sudden overwhelming rush. The lucky writer whose ideas in the past have patiently taken their place in line may discover that only partway into his new novel, he is inexplicably in love with an idea for still another book.

Whether the idea came to you in your sleep or you had to go looking for it, whether you fell in love with it at once or only over a course of time, the "right" idea draws from you such eagerness that you can scarcely think of anything else. Small fragments of plots and characters and themes rub against each other until they kindle the spark that will soon start the whole process going. Your novel is the last thought in your head before going to sleep at night, the first thing on your mind in the morning. You may find yourself waking early, impatient to get on with your work. It will take most of your energy, require your fiercest concentration, and become the focal point of your life.

This is how a book begins.

❧ 2

Writing from Your Roots

I'VE ALWAYS WANTED to write mysteries, but I've led such a boring life," a woman confided once. "The only thing I know about is real estate, and what could I do with that?"

Was she joking? I wondered. Anyone who knows about real estate knows something about houses and the way people live. She knows the real-estate jargon that would give such a novel authenticity. She knows marketing and advertising, the eccentricities of various customers, and what people look for in a home.

Suppose a cleaning crew enters a vacant house and finds: (a) a suicide note; (b) blood; (c) a body? Suppose a new client asks for a secluded home far out in the country with an elaborate security system and a soundproof basement without windows? Suppose a female real estate agent takes a new client to see a house, and the moment they are inside, he takes her hostage? Or what if one particular house has sold twice in the last three years, and in each instance, the wife in the family died a sudden, horrible death? It's a matter of using an ordinary situation and carrying it one step further, the old technique of "What if?"

The gold mine within ourselves

Willa Cather said, "Let your fiction grow out of the land beneath your feet." And again, "The years from eight to fifteen are the formative period in a writer's life." When I first read this, years ago, I could not see how it applied to me. It wasn't that there was nothing to write about back in the Midwest; we simply didn't stay in one place long enough to put down roots. The land beneath *my* feet was constantly changing. In *Crazy Love* I wrote:

Mine was the most ordinary family in the entire Midwest. Whenever people wrote about middle-class values, mores, income, or politics, that was my family they were talking about. A walking Norman Rockwell portfolio, that was us. We were descended on both sides from a long line of teachers, preachers, and farmers. My father worked for various companies, beginning with H.J. Heinz in the Depression, symbolized by a giant pickle. All through our childhood he was so loyal that I didn't discover Campbell's soups until I was married. As he changed jobs, we changed houses, and by the time I entered high school, we had lived in eight different neighborhoods, stretching across Indiana, Illinois, and Iowa. And that's where our personalities developed. Like the roads in Iowa as seen from a plane, all coming together at perfect right angles, the men and women of American gothic lived their lives square and true. . . .

It was not just the five of us—mother, father, three children—who were ordinary, however. Counting all blood relatives on both sides—forty-four aunts, uncles, cousins, and grandparents—no one had ever been in jail. No one had ever been arrested, molested, or raped. No one had ever had heart disease, diabetes, or tuberculosis. No one got his picture in *Look* or *Life*. When two of my uncles founded a manufacturing company for heavy equipment, we finally had a success story to recount again and again over the ham and biscuits at family reunions. And when one of my aunts married a man who later robbed this company (he was apprehended making his getaway at seven miles an hour in the huge orange crane he had stolen), we had a scandal, too, of our very own.

In my formative years, I frequently vacationed at either of my grandparents' homes. If we drove west to Iowa, we drove along flat boring farmland with peaceful cows, endlessly chewing. There my world was bordered by cornfields and fences, and ruled by my maternal German-Scottish grandmother, without emotion or fuss. If we headed east to Maryland, however, the land became mysterious and hilly about the time we reached Pittsburgh. From then on, the terrain was rolling, the roads curving, and we would arrive at last at the home of my paternal grandparents, who had migrated from Mississippi, bringing the humid, suffocating climate of inbred warmth and gossip along with them.

In Marbury, Maryland, I found that I could walk almost anywhere I wanted to go—to the one-room post-office, the firehouse, a small grocery, the neighbors, or the church where my grandfather was pastor. For the first time in my life, I had a town I could encompass on foot, roads I could connect, faces that attached themselves to names I heard mentioned over the supper table. My grandmother, the neighborhood midwife, knew almost everyone in Marbury, and claimed to have delivered most of its children.

It wasn't until years later, on a nostalgic drive back to Marbury, that I decided to set my first novel for adults, *Revelations*, there. And it was some years after that, when I set a second novel in Maryland, and then a third, that I realized this small southern town had worked its way into my blood. Driving along its one-lane roads, canopied with trees that opened up occasionally for a tobacco field, then closed again, past signs saying, *Turkey Shoot, Every Sunday, Eleven till Three* or *Jesus Saves and Heals*, I could

hear my grandparents' southern voices, the drawl of the
hired man, the admonitions, complaints, and blessings.
At the time I was experiencing it, however, and for many
years afterward, it all seemed so ordinary. Certainly I
knew that most grandmothers did not take wards of the
state into their homes and care for them—elderly patients
like Sister Ozzie and the dysphasic Mr. Schmidt in my book
A String of Chances—but as a self-conscious teen-ager, I
found this to be humiliating.

I knew, too, that not all grandfathers were ministers, but
I was a little embarrassed about mine. Grandfather Reynolds was not, after all, the graduate of a divinity school. He
had picked up his theological training in the same way that
my grandmother picked up her nursing expertise, and they
always seemed terribly "backwoods." I wonder now why it
took me so long to realize how valuable all of this would be
to me some day.

Writing what you know
Scratch the surface of any writing course and somewhere
in the lectures or readings you are bound to come across the
advice to "write what you know." Most of us look for something unusual we might know a lot about—sailing, a serious
car accident, an alcoholic parent, beauty contests, a tor-
nado, diamonds. These subjects are fine if they are really in
your blood, but what if you have had a rather normal family,
no catastrophic events, and no unusual hobbies or achieve-
ments? Where do you begin then?

With yourself. For starters, describe the room where you
sleep—the location of the windows, the shape of the mirror,
the marks on the walls, the lines on the ceiling, the dust on
the baseboard, the tangle of belts on a nail in the closet. . .
anything at all that will make the occupant of this room real

to the reader. What can we surmise about this person from the type of magazines there by the bed, the number of pillows, the comforter thrown carelessly over the trunk, the receipts on the dresser top, the shirt with the perspiration stains?

Or is this, instead, the room of a most meticulous person, with a place for everything and everything in its place? *What if* Jane, a perfectionistic young woman, advertises for a roommate and gets someone even more compulsive and obsessively neat than she? Suppose that, over a period of time and through their experiences together, Jane sees herself in Caroline; she sees someone who wants to control not only her surroundings, but her friends as well—everyone else must meet her standards. She begins to get a sense of how rigid she has been, and realizes that her high expectations are robbing her of the normal give-and-take of friendship.

What do you do best? What is the worst thing that ever happened to you? In what ways do your relatives seem different from other people? Where have you lived that you weren't happy? If you could change one thing about yourself, what would it be? So often we fail to see the gold mine inside ourselves. We look everywhere else for a story, not realizing that the book that only we can write was inside us all the time.

"But I don't really like myself much," protests one person.

Another confides, "There are things about my marriage I would prefer others didn't know."

Of course there are things you will not want to write about in detail. Of course there are privacies to be respected, secrets to be kept. A little mystery is a good thing. So write about a main character who does not seem to like herself much, but whose reasons need not be yours. Write about what it is like to have to guard a secret, and what happens when that secret gets out, though it need not be *your* secret.

What about a man who so carefully guards his wife's past that he becomes a recluse; he spoils his own chances for happiness only to discover in the end that the community knew about his wife's early indiscretions all the time and accepted her as she was? What about a woman who so dislikes herself that she changes everything—her face, figure, personality, her name, even—and then discovers that she was a better person the way she was before? We can use real feelings, if not facts; motives, it not acts; a trait, if not every revealing characteristic of those we know.

This is where skill is called for, in the weaving of the story fabric with all its assorted threads. This is what we yearn to do well as writers, extending reality to include other events, other people, and achieving that perfect blend.

Experiences that were terrible in an author's own life may become less so in his manuscript because they are intertwined with circumstances and options that were not open to him in reality or which, unhappily, he did not consider at the time. Or a writer may decide to use a trauma from his own life that actually turned out well, but he invents a different ending on paper just to see what will come of it. An author, in fact, may write about something that has not yet happened to him, but which he fears may happen, just to see if he could cope. Or he may bring out into the open a past tragedy, finding a catharsis in writing about it.

On the other hand, there are many details from real life we will not want to change in our novels. The very ordinariness of a food-splattered wall above the stove, for example, will ring a bell with anyone who has ever cooked. The odd sneaker lying under the coffee table will strike a familiar note to any parent. The contorted face of a woman refusing to let the tears come at her mother's burial, or the superficial banter of neighborhood men working in their yards on a Saturday are ordinary, one might say, but they contribute the very details that add richness to a book and make it ring true.

Finding the universal note

It is the universality in theme, as well as detail, that gives a novel meaning and makes it memorable. Themes, like details, can be very ordinary; it is the way the writer handles them that makes them special.

If you sometimes confuse plot with theme, keep the two elements separate by thinking of theme as what the story is about, and plot as the situation that brings it into focus. You might think of theme as the message of the story—the lesson to be learned, the question that is asked, or what it is the author is trying to tell us about life and the human condition. Plot is the action by which this truth will be demonstrated.

In *A String of Chances*, for example, the theme is how young people cope when they must decide which of their parents' values they will adopt, and which they will discard. When you love your parents, but disagree with them, how do you grow up without growing away? As the daughter of a fundamentalist preacher, Evie has this problem in the book. This is the theme. But it is the plot that brings this problem to a head: the crib death of a cousin's infant son, whom Evie has grown to love. When her father tries to explain to her that it is all a part of God's mysterious plan, Evie realizes that for her this does not answer the "Why?" at all, and lashes out at her father and his teachings.

Theme is what readers think about long after they've finished a book. What *meaning* did it have? What was it that really mattered? What is it the author wants most to share?

It may be an idea that the author considers original: for instance, that men are more likely to marry a mother-figure than women are to marry father-figures. Or vice versa. The theme may be a universal truth not original at all, but difficult to accept: death is final.

The theme may be simply one of life's ordinary lessons that has particular meaning for the author: the realization that parents are people with problems too, and tend to hand them down—like family heirlooms—to the next generation. Perhaps the lesson is that there is no such thing as real security, that all you can count on is change.

Some authors have no particular theme in mind until they get to know their characters, see them interact on stage. Only then do they discover what their characters' problems are, and hence, what the theme of the novel will be.

Whatever you choose as your theme, it must have meaning for you; you don't simply select it at random or because you think it might be popular. Laments Isaac Bashevis Singer: "The Zionists would like me to preach Zionism, the Socialists would like me to preach socialism. The homosexuals would like that I should all the time praise homosexuality. 'Or why don't you write about women's liberation?' they say. They assume that a writer should sit there and look out for every vogue and immediately there should be a novel about it. I prefer to write about the world which I knew, which I know best. . . . This is enough for me."

John Updike insists that "there has to be an irritation that makes you want to cry out. All fiction is, in a funny way, protest fiction."

However it is chosen, the theme must subtly permeate the story—a faint brush stroke there on the page, a whisper between the lines. The novels and plays and movies that live are those that stimulate discussion once they are over, that provoke controversy, that make the readers or the audience contribute something of themselves in order to get the point. In other words, the thoughtful writer will leave something to readers' imaginations, allowing them to put in the final piece of the puzzle. This makes for a more satisfying reading experience than if the author spells out heavy-handedly what the novel is all about.

If, for example, your theme is that men are more likely to marry women like their mothers than women are to marry men like their fathers, you may create a family consisting of a domineering mother, a quiet, passive father, three sons, and a daughter. You may touch upon these young people's lives in their teens and through their early marriages to show that after discarding wives whom the reader might deem perfectly suitable, two of the sons marry women who tend to decide things for them. One son stays married, but sullen, to a woman who tried without success to please him. The daughter, who married a loud-mouthed extrovert as her first choice, is still happily married.

Nowhere do you actually state your theme. The plot has many strands. But slowly the reader comes to the conclusion that after all the antagonism between the sons and their mother when they were younger, they still developed a need for her dominance in their lives, while the daughter, who was also rebellious against her too-passive dad, did not want to duplicate his personality in a husband. And if, after all this, you still believe in your theme or are simply curious enough to want to play with it and see where it leads, you will drop hints throughout the novel as to what needs males may have for extra nurturing that females do not. There is also the possibility you will decide the whole thing is ludicrous and toss it out. That happens, too.

Taking the road not taken

When we write a novel, we are inviting the reader to be part of the experience because, in the final analysis, the book belongs to the reader; the novel's meaning is whatever he may make of it. He may, of course, see something other than what the author intended. The character who was dearest to the author's heart may seem selfish or vacillating to the reader. But readers are as entitled to their interpretation of the characters and events in the novel as the author is to his.

When we consider our parents, our past, our mistakes, our successes and what we imagine our future to be, we can see many roads not taken, many decisions not made. We can't relive our lives, but we can rework them through fiction. We can put our characters through imaginary paces and see what would have happened had we chosen a different route. We can trade one problem for another, we can become single again or, if single, become married and take on a houseful of children. We are trying on many hats, and the reader is doing the same.

It is only when the book is published that we find out just how many different things it was to different people. One reader may feel that Helen's walking out on her aged mother was sadistic and cruel, while another may be relieved that Helen finally got up her nerve to break away. Reader A may look at a novel's ending as the protagonist's failure, while Reader B sees courage and hope. The author himself may have had something more subtle in mind than either failure or hope—the vagaries of life, perhaps, the randomness of circumstance. He was writing from something in his life that was beyond the experience of either reader A or B.

The list of reasons we write what we do is endless; it is

surpassed only by the reasons we write at all. For me, the urge to create a story is a physical thing—something I just must do. If I don't write every day, I feel like those sour-faced people in commercials who suffer from irregularity. I can't explain it better than that.

We can change our names, our vocations, our addresses, our spouses, but we cannot ever, even for an instant, physically leave our bodies and become someone else. We are all prisoners forever inside our own skins. The only way out is through the imagination.

As the novelist Anne Tyler put it, "I write because I want more than one life; I insist on a wider selection. It's greed, plain and simple."

🌀 3

Beginnings

YOU'VE GOT AN IDEA that includes a story line. Whenever you think about it, you add a little more, and the excitement grows. You're getting to the place where everything you see or hear or feel seems grist for the mill. *Maybe I can use it* becomes your dominant thought.

At what point do you begin the actual writing? What groundwork should be laid ahead of time that may save you grief later on?

An idea for a book may strike with such force that you are unable to do almost anything else until something—however sketchy— is down on paper. Just starting the first paragraph may provide enough release to give you the feeling of having "begun," and you can be more relaxed about the rest.

Or you may take notes for weeks—months, even—letting the story gradually pick up speed until one day you discover that you want to begin the writing more than anything else, and so you do.

Not all authors use the same starting place. Some begin with a character so strong that the plot seems secondary. The book opens with the protagonist in a particular situation, and the author has only the vaguest notion of where the plot is going. Though some writers are enormously successful in simply allowing the characters to lead, there are many wrong turns these characters might take if they have no road map or at least some signposts along the way.

But Tom Stoppard, the playwright, has said that *his* biggest problem is deciding how to populate his work. The ideas come first and the characters follow, often slowly. The time of greatest anxiety, he claims, is getting as far as page one.

There are hints and helps to the writer beginning a novel, but no magic formula. For most of us, it is a process of trial and error.

Titles

A book's title is important because it can help entice a reader. The title may, in fact, be the only advertisement your novel is going to get. If it is displayed in bookstores, it may be on a shelf, spine out, so that not even the cover art will be visible, and all the browser is going to see is the title.

After weeks of agonizing, after writing page after page of possibilities, after trying them out on friends, you may think you have found the perfect title and then, when you check *Books in Print*, discover that there are already two novels by that name. And while a title cannot be copyrighted, it's better not to use one currently in print.

Of course it's wonderful to have a catchy title when you submit your manuscript to a publisher, but you need not spend an enormous amount of time on it because, in all probability, an editor will suggest another. Unless you can't seem to begin the first paragraph of a novel until you have a working title, you may want to wait until the book is written, then look for the phrase or single word that most aptly sums it up.

In any case, titles depend very much on personal taste.

Perhaps the best you can do is to have a list of second choices available, should the title you want be rejected, and hope that one of them will suit your publishers.

The moment of truth

The terror of seeing that blank piece of paper staring at you from your typewriter, or that green cursor on your computer screen awaiting your instructions, can be almost paralyzing. This is the moment you say you have been awaiting for months or even years if you only had the time. All those wonderful ideas and bits of dialogue and settings and subplots, rolling over and over in your mind. It is not at all unusual for writers to sit down at their desks, stare at their typewriters, and suddenly decide to clean out their file drawers first, *then* begin. We are all frightened that our first sentence may prove that those many months of research, preparation, and thinking produced nothing worthwhile. William Styron talks about it as "plunging into unknown territory not really knowing whether you're going to come out alive."

There are several ways to get over this hump, and good reasons for choosing each. You may decide to write the entire novel quickly just as the words come to you, getting a sense of the mood and characters and pace, so that you have a framework on which to build. Then you will want to revise again and again, sure, at least, of where the story's headed. Since you have written hastily, you will not be out much if you make major changes during the revisions. A disadvantage of this method is that if you give little time to artistry on this preliminary draft, you may decide, after you have reread the first twenty pages, that this is the most boring story about the world's most boring person, and toss the whole thing out.

On the other hand, you may feel that you want each

sentence well written before you go on to the next; then you won't have to do as much rewriting later. This may work if the whole book, scene by scene, rolls by in front of your eyes like a movie. The advantage here is that the more true-to-life your characters become early on, the more easily the story will flow; the better you know your region and local color, the more naturally your characters will interact with it. Your motivation is high because you see right from the beginning how well things are going. Since many of us may not know what is going to happen in scene four until we write scenes one, two, and three, however, this plan is not for everyone. And if, halfway through the book, you decide on major changes, this means that some of those scenes on which you spent hours or weeks must be done over.

Susan Fromberg Schaeffer says, "I don't start to write until I know what the book is about from beginning to end, scene by scene. When I actually begin writing, something strange happens. I become enveloped in a kind of conflagration, a burning to get the book out of my system. I write the book all the way through, stopping as little as possible. I sleep only two or three hours a night. All the energy I might release if I wrote a little at a time builds up and spills out almost beyond my control. I acquire a kind of immunity, but after each book is finished, I always get sick." (Once recovered, she completely retypes the book, making revisions as she goes.)

At the opposite extreme is Lore Segal, who took seven years to write the 177 pages of *Lucinella*. And Gustave Flaubert who, even as he grew weary with the writing of *Madame Bovary*, which took four and a half years, refused to "hurry up by a single second a sentence that isn't ripe."

Most of us devise an individual method somewhere between these two extremes. The beginning novelist may prefer to write the first chapter quickly, not worrying too much about the perfect word or exact phrase, and then revise it once or twice before going on to chapter two. This gives him the advantage of getting a start without being paralyzed by concerns for perfection, but it requires more serious editing and planning in the second and third drafts before proceeding with the rest of the book.

There is certainly no harm in trying a different method from time to time. Writers, like everyone else, do change; those who claimed they could never write on a word processor often discover, to their amazement, that they can. Authors who have always used a typewriter sometimes find, when they reach a difficult passage, that reverting to pen and paper does the trick.

But if ideas do not flow as well using someone else's method, then do what works for you, even if it means writing a page at a time, taking it through seven or eight drafts, and then going on to the next one.

The opening paragraph

What you *must* do sooner or later in that opening paragraph, however, is to lure the reader in. Not in your first draft, necessarily, or even the second or third, but eventually.

Think of your first paragraph as the show window in a department store, and your opening sentence as the main attraction on display. Whether the reader walks on by or stops to ponder is largely up to you.

How Richard Wharton found himself standing in Times Square wearing only his socks, he really didn't know, may grab almost anyone. It would be a marvelous opening sentence, but only if it were intrinsic to the story. If Richard *wasn't* standing there in only his socks, but merely dreamed that he was, and the dream has very little to do with what happens next, then the author has used deceptive advertising.

Beginning writers may find it difficult to jump right into their plots, because they realize that at some point they must explain how their characters got there, and it seems easier just to start at the beginning. But bookstores really don't need another novel that begins with the protagonist getting out of bed in the morning and reminiscing about all of the things that readers need to know regarding his past. We can be more creative than that.

It's scary, perhaps, but that first sentence must carry more weight than almost any other sentence in the book. It does not have to be eloquent or profound or amusing or titillating, but it must, in some way, touch the heart of the story; it must also be a finger beckoning, urging the reader in. Author Gloria Naylor explains it this way: "One should be able to return to the first sentence of a novel and find the resonances of the entire work. That first sentence is the DNA, spawning the second sentence, the second the third."

What would attract *you* to your book? Is there one sentence that would both entice and give you a sense of the story to come? With what scene could you begin that would be interesting enough to hold the reader's attention on into chapter two, even if you must backtrack later on?

By the time the reader has finished the first page of your novel, he should have some idea, however slight, of the kind of book this is going to be—a mystery, a farce, a sardonic tale, a realistic human drama. . . . He should also have a hint as to what type of person the central character is. But you do not have to lay all your cards on the table on that first page. You don't have to give a complete description of the heroine's face and body and home and husband and occupation and where she went to school.

We have all had the experience, on meeting someone for the first time, of hearing him tell far more about himself than we wanted to know. Because he allows us no unanswered questions, he robs himself of mystery and hence of interest. Every novel needs a bit of mystery, a question mark, to lure readers on.

It can be helpful, before you begin writing, to jot down what is most important for your readers to learn in the first paragraph, the first page, and the first scene. Is it crucial for them to know right from the start in what region this story takes place? Can you allude to the conflict without having to describe it in detail?

You'll want to choose selectively from among the most interesting facets of your novel. The first paragraph is like the overture to a symphony—a taste of things to come—without dwelling too long on any one theme or conflict. But you will include only the most necessary things. You certainly do not want a paragraph that begins, *Lorraine Sibley, age 32, second vice-president of Continental Savings and Loan, put in a call to her North Shore apartment to see if her husband Ted, a tennis pro, was home yet and, getting no answer, hung up, relieved, running one slim, manicured hand through the tangles of her reddish-blond hair, and wondered how she would ever tell him that Stephanie, their daughter, was not his.*

The most important, most interesting information in that paragraph is that Stephanie is not Ted's daughter, he doesn't know it, and for some reason Lorraine now feels obliged or forced to tell him. Next in importance is the fact that Lorraine is a business woman; hence she might have some professional reason to want to keep this information under wraps. This is what will grab the reader—not Lorraine's exact position in the company or her age or the color of her hair. Nor do we need to know in this first paragraph where she lives. All these things can come out later. First things first: *Lorraine Sibley called home from the executive lounge and, getting no answer, wondered how she would tell her husband that their daughter was not his.*

It is not just the information that is conveyed in the first paragraph of a novel that is crucial, but how it is conveyed. The sentences should have a subtle rhythm all their own. Read your paragraph aloud to see what clicks, what jars, and how to make the sentences go more smoothly. Do they read in a sing-song manner because you have too many commas? Do too many of the words sound alike, ending in "er" or "ing"? Are the sentences precise and stiff, the words too pedantic?

Some first paragraphs, of course, are intended to shock. Your story may begin abruptly, with the sharp crack of a rifle and the sound of hurried footsteps. But whatever effect you wish to evoke in your opening paragraph, the writing must be done with skill and grace. There should be a natural flow to the words that suits the mood and action, and there is no better test than to read the paragraph aloud again and again. Having succeeded at last in doing what you wanted to do on your first page, you now have a model for the remaining pages of your story, and you will, of course, give the same care and attention to each of them.

Looking ahead

As you work on your novel, there are going to be many ideas that come to you at odd times, and it will be helpful to keep notebooks handy—a large one with compartments for maps, articles, and newspaper clippings, and a smaller notebook to carry in a pocket when you are not at home to jot down that phrase that strikes suddenly, that line of dialogue, that description of a field, the subplot that just occurred to you.

It's also useful to write down for constant referral the theme and plot of your book. This may seem ridiculously elementary. If, after all, you have been thinking about this book for two years, surely you are not going to forget the theme and plot in the writing of it, are you?

Not exactly. But as a plot grows and picks up subplots, as characters who you didn't even know had tickets come on board, you can find your novel sailing off on a tangent. You may have started a book about the relationship between a young man and his father, but when the ex-wife comes into the picture, you can suddenly find, halfway through, that the young man hasn't been seen or heard from since chapter six; the book has become, instead, a commentary on ex-wives.

You may want to draw up an outline of your novel before you begin, dividing it into the approximate number of chapters, with the most crucial scenes listed per chapter. Or a simple summary of the novel will prove helpful, not only to see—in black and white—that there is indeed a plot in there somewhere, but to make sure that it builds toward a climax and that you don't muck about too long in the story afterwards.

For Joyce Carol Oates, who writes incessantly, each work is preceded by months of daydreaming, working it out in her head. "I know the ending, I know the last paragraph, I know what's going through this person's mind," she says. "But I have to find the words to get into it."

Before you begin your novel you should have, if nothing else, some idea of the opening, the climax, the ending, and a few major events that will take place along the way. These are not engraved in stone, of course. You may decide later to start your book with chapter two. Or when you get to the climax stated in your outline, a better one might come to mind. You need to be flexible enough to "go with the flow" when you feel the current strongly, but don't just jump in feet first without having a fairly good notion of where you are headed.

A summary is also useful to refer to again and again as you write the novel. Does it read like a capsulized review of a book you would want to buy? Do you see in it suspense? Conflict? An unusual situation or character? A setting that rings true?

This is a good place to make changes before you go any further. After reading your summary, does it seem too heavy—too much of a "downer"? Perhaps this can't be helped; this is the kind of novel you meant it to be, and there is not much room for levity. In such a case, perhaps you hope that the viewpoint or the characters will be the book's saving grace, and you prefer to take your chances. You may think of a way later on to add lightness or even a sardonic kind of humor to give your reader moments of respite, a chance to catch his breath before he moves on.

You may decide, when you read your summary, that it seems much too melodramatic, and you will make a mental note to write sparingly, keeping a firm hand on the emotional reins. Or your summary may sound too much like stage directions—the characters did this and that—without much feeling at all. So you will write in the margin of your summary: *with feeling.*

It is in the summary that you may discover you are not sure what the climactic scene will be; that the ending seems to fall on its face, as you have described it; that there is too much action, too little action, that the plot or theme sounds too cerebral or not insightful enough. While it is true that none of these criticisms may turn out to be valid once you are into the actual writing, the fact that you get these vibes when you read your summary points to things you must watch out for, traps you may have set for yourself, things you may have overlooked.

The following, for example, may be one whale of a plot: *A man carefully plans his sister's murder down to the last detail, with methods to cover his tracks, but in the end, she uses his own plan to kill him.* You may find, when you read your summary, that you have devised the most cunning murder possible; for every step the man takes, he has an alibi. What you do not have, you may discover when you begin writing the story itself, is motivation. You have only a vague idea why he hates his sister so much that he wants to kill her. Unless his motivation is clear, unless your readers can feel what the protagonist is feeling, however bizarre or unreasonable or sick, they simply will not be able to get too deeply into the story. Furthermore, if the sister *is* so despicable that readers think she deserves to die, then how will they feel when she outwits him?

These basic problems can usually be detected and solved by reading a summary over objectively and asking yourself questions. Let nothing slip by you. If you see a potential problem, don't wait until you get to that point in the writing to do something about it. Now is the time to act like a prosecuting attorney: Why did he do that? How long has he been feeling this way? Why doesn't he do something else? The more you work out in advance, the easier the writing will go and the less an editor will have to argue about later.

๔ 4

Problems of Plot

PLOT RARELY PRESENTS ITSELF to the writer in complete form with beginning, climax, and denouement. Most often it has its origin as an interesting set of circumstances that these particular characters might find themselves in. Only as the author plays with this situation, works with it, asking that perpetual "What if. . . ?" does the plot come into focus.

The more you toy with it, of course, the more it changes—frequently into something quite different from what you started with. Never mind. You wouldn't be the first writer to change plots in midstream, or to discover that your major theme was different from what you had thought. And this is all right. It may, in fact, be a far better plot with a much stronger theme.

But unless your story is then securely attached to the new theme or plot, you may find when you are through that the novel is murky. Your first form rejection letter may have a scribbled question at the end that asks, "What exactly are you trying to say?"

The plot in a nutshell

It is often useful to write down, in twenty-five words or less, what the action, or the main happening in your novel, will be. What, in a nutshell, is the plot, as opposed to theme? Keep this before you and refer to it often. For example: "When a family secret is revealed, a young man and his father discover that they share much more than they had thought." If you can think of nothing more vital for a reader to know than this, then you have the necessary seeds of your book.

Who are the central characters? *The young man and his father.* If this is your main focus, you can create other marvelous characters, of course, but don't allow them to detract from the father and son.

What is the main theme? It could be any number of topics, but perhaps in this instance it is *The importance of family continuity—the father as a link to the son's past, the son as the father's link to the future.* You may have several other serious things you want to say, and including them is permissible as long as the main theme stays predominant and fits with the plot like a hand in a glove. They must seem to have been made for each other.

What is the main climax? *The way the father and son interract and change when the family secret is revealed.* The revelation may be, in fact, one of the most dramatic scenes in the book. Or it may be very low key, and it is the aftereffects that provide the fireworks.

And what are possible subplots? *Any separate story line that helps advance the main plot but does not steal the show.* The part the young man's mother plays, for one. Perhaps she and the father are estranged. Perhaps she has kept the secret, whatever it is, in the hope that the son would remain closer to her than he is to the father.

Another subplot may be the young man's girlfriend and their relationship in the midst of all this stress. Perhaps, in a neat twist near the end, it will be the girlfriend who discovers the secret and inadvertently reveals it at a family gathering.

Subplots are like smaller streams all feeding into a river.

Near the end of their voyage, the waters have merged, but for a while each stream keeps its own identity. Subplots within a novel are often so interesting that the author could write separate books about them alone. And some authors do, taking the characters and situation that played a minor role in one book and giving them star billing in a new novel.

What makes a good plot? Flannery O'Connor said all good stories are about a character's changing. If he were stable, she said, there wouldn't be any story. It may not necessarily be change for the better, of course; but *something must happen that makes this week or this month or this year in the life of your main character different from any other time in his life, or why write about it at all?* Why did you select this situation to write about if it was not a circumstance that made a difference?

Is your protagonist facing a crisis? Must he make a difficult choice? Is he an unemployed man, perhaps, who—to make the situation more crucial—has a sick wife? And when he finally, desperately, lands a job, discovers he is being asked to do something that goes against his own moral code?

Conflict

For a novel to have conflict, the leading character must face a problem that is important—critical, even—for him to solve. And he must solve it himself without the intervention of God, an anonymous letter, or an inheritance. There should be obstacles, also, to overcome along the way. It's not enough for Belinda Harrison, at the news of her brother's death, to give up her socialite life in 1863 to travel west to take over his homestead in Kansas; getting there has to be half the problem, with hair-raising incidents of all kinds. And then what if, arriving at last, she finds his cabin burned to the ground? Figuratively speaking, we not only get our heroine up a creek without a paddle, but we devise a hailstorm, too.

But it won't do merely to have an act of providence strike a character in your story and then see how she reacts to it. This burden must be especially difficult for her, in particular, to bear. Suppose the protagonist is a minister who preaches that accidents are not accidents at all, but the will of God against those who disobey His teachings; and then the minister's own beloved wife is paralyzed from the neck down in an auto accident.

Such a circumstance makes the climax all the more electrifying. The reader is far less likely to say, "Well, too bad, but so what?"

It is even better if the burden does not just fall out of the blue, but is brought on in part by the main character himself: the stern, unbending president of a college has held up his daughter as the reluctant role model for her peers; he shows no mercy to students or faculty who do not live up to his moral standards. Suppose, then, he discovers that his daughter is having an affair with a member of the college football team.

Conflicts are not just hurdles thrown in the character's way; each must pit him against something within himself. If he must climb this particular mountain to rescue a friend, for example, then give him the additional burden of having to overcome a fear of heights. Even better if it is not a friend he is required to rescue, but a mortal enemy. If the conflict is between two estranged parents each battling for custody of their child, then make them painfully aware that in many ways the other person would be the better parent. Face to face in court, each confronts his own secret misgivings about whether he is doing the right thing.

A hurricane bearing down on a coastal town where an old

man refuses to leave his mobile home makes for a dramatic situation. The drama is heightened as he barricades himself inside the trailer and will not open the door to rescue officials. A son is sent for to talk the old man out of his obstinacy, and here the real conflict emerges: The son has been so busy with his own life all these years that the father has created a little world for himself inside his trailer and is loathe to leave it. Now, with winds howling and the waters rising, the son must convince the old man that he does have a place in his son's life, that he is needed and wanted.

The hook

What is the "hook" in your story going to be? What, in other words, is going to pull your readers through the novel, keep them turning the pages, and make them want to know more?

Perhaps this is a novel about a man who, despite all advice, takes his young wife to Alaska to start a small business as a bush pilot. And the odds against him are so great that the reader wonders, from one page to the next, whether he is ever going to make it, as disaster after disaster befalls him. The suspense will be all the greater if there is more than an ordinary reason why he must succeed (he is a former convict, for example, truly reformed, but no one will give him a chance).

It may be that from the opening of the novel, readers know what will happen; it may be that you, the author, have told them that a year after the ex-convict moved to Alaska, his young wife was dead, and the suspense lies in guessing *how* it happened, or *why*.

Perhaps the tension comes from trying to guess which of two choices your central character will make, or in guessing whether or not he will garner the strength needed to face an obstacle that, until now, seemed impossible to overcome.

Suppose there is a crippled man being cared for by his selfish and somewhat sadistic brother. The readers know he should leave; *he* knows he should leave, but he is so dependent on his brother, how would he manage if he did? Whether in the character or the plot or the situation or the mood, there must be suspense in the novel. You must keep your readers guessing. You must keep the level of tension high enough to make each chapter more than just another interesting revelation about your character, or just another humorous episode in his life. Somewhere, fairly close to the beginning of your book, the reader must sense that there is a question mark hanging over your protagonist, that something about his life is unsettled, that there is a decision or a choice to be made, or a problem to be solved, and that upon this decision or choice rest the futures or fortunes of several other characters as well.

In other words, the main problem must have repercussions. The reader must sense that he has not merely stepped into the first chapter of a book, but into a tangled web of emotions and conflicts that are not going to be easily resolved.

If the ex-convict starts a bush pilot business and fails, his wife may leave him, and he may return to crime. Meanwhile some of his prison buddies find out where he is and decide to freeload off him for a while, creating problems in his business, ill will from the neighbors, and tension between him and his wife.

If the crippled man leaves his brother's house, not only will he have to fend for himself, but he will be leaving the one person who really loves him, his five-year-old nephew. If solutions seem too easy in your novel, readers may decide that they don't need to read any further.

You do not, should not, of course, delineate all the problems at the outset. But every chapter must leave enough questions about your plot in the reader's mind so that even when he is not reading your novel, he will think about it and can't wait to pick up the book again to see whether or not his hunch was right.

"How on earth will he get out of that one?" is a question your reader will quite naturally ask of the detective who has just hailed a taxi and finds himself beside a man who has been trying to kill him.

But it's not only detective novels and mysteries that need suspense. Even humorous novels must have hooks. What will the beloved gentleman do next? readers wonder, as each thing an elderly man forgets is more serious than the one before. And finally, humor turns to alarm when he drives his four grandchildren to the fair and, halfway home, discovers there are only three in the back seat.

There is probably not a novel written that does not have a counterpart somewhere—possibly several of them. Jealousy and revenge, filial ingratitude, love versus duty—every emotion and conflict and situation has already been done. Almost any published author knows that as soon as he begins to write his novel, he may find a similar book on the market. Perhaps the main characters in both novels have the same first names and work at the same occupation; perhaps your protagonist faces the same family problem as in someone else's novel. Such similarities cannot be helped. But if you are writing from what is unique within yourself, it will show in your manuscript, and an editor will not mind that it has been done before because you are doing it in a new way.

Credibility

Plot is often the most difficult part of writing a novel. You solve one problem only to discover that, in its solution, you have created two more. Or you find that your intricately woven web does not take into account the climate in the area or the age of the leading character or the traditions of a particular group. Then you must think through your plot still again. When an author is praised for a book that "flows," for a plot that is uncontrived, he offers silent thanks that all his effort and string-pulling were not discovered, for a novel is nothing if not contrived. Characters are moved and manipulated, seasons are chosen, locations are researched, motives are analyzed, but all this must be done so skillfully that it never detracts from the story. The reader must believe that what happens in your novel was exactly the way it could happen, not a one-in-a-million chance.

Nobody said that writing is easy.

It may help to imagine an editor or instructor reading your novel or summary—someone whose opinion you trust. Would this person say, do you think, that the plot has been done a hundred times, or would he say that what you intend to do with it, as evidenced in your summary, seems a fresh approach?

Would an editor say, given the plot as outlined, that the conclusion is predictable? The reader must feel, when he has closed the book, that while he might have guessed its conclusion, he was still taken somewhat by surprise at exactly the way it was done. Or in retrospect, that he found it satisfying and acceptable. But he must not say that not only was he surprised and could never have predicted it in a thousand years, but it is much too implausible—that human beings just don't act that way, or that for the book to have ended as you've ended it, too many unlikely things must have occurred. In other words, the ending appears contrived.

"But this actually happened!" is no defense. If we read a newspaper account of some unusual occurrence, we believe it because it was witnessed and reported. But if we read the same thing in fiction, we may dismiss it as unbelievable. "Fact or fiction, fiction or fact. Which stops where, and how much to put in of each?" asks author Gail Godwin. "At what point does regurgitated autobiography graduate into memory shaped by art? How do you know when to stop telling it as it is, or was, and make it into what it ought to be—or what would make it a better story?"

We sometimes build our climax on a prior event that proves incredible. Everything seemed to be working fine in a manuscript, one author discovered, until he remembered that such a trip would not have been planned during the monsoon season; things were going along splendidly in chapter two, another writer found, until he realized that a woman with bronchial pneumonia would probably not have done what his character did; still another thought that everything in *his* novel was a neat, tidy package until he concluded that Ned could not have let the horse out of the barn without realizing that the mare down the road was in heat. In other words, the results that followed were contrived.

Of all the facets that should be taken into account early on in the writing of your novel, plot is the one that must be most firmly grounded. You will need to go over it again and again, thinking ahead, making sure that everything follows in a natural sequence, and that holes are filled in eventually with flashbacks.

No matter how much planning you do, however—as in the building of a house—you will discover during the construction of your story that there are unforeseen problems and unexpected developments. But if the plot is sound and solid, you may make the necessary changes, knowing that your foundation will hold.

⚜ 5

When Characters Come Alive

FOR MANY WRITERS, the most wonderful moment of
writing—the thing that gives them the "high"—is that
moment a character comes to life on paper. This is what all
the rest of the work was for—the worry, the months and
months of thinking, the notes, the research. Before then,
your invented protagonist was just someone in the back of
your head, a paragraph in a scribbled summary, a few pages
of description in a notebook, but suddenly here he is, someone you'd swear that you knew before. What brings about
this transformation?

Avoiding stereotypes

One of the first things you should consider when characters come to mind is to avoid making them into stereotypes.
Of course there are pot-bellied men who sit on doorsteps in
their undershirts and drink beer; of course there are pink-
cheeked mums who wear aprons and bake apple pies, and
there are intellectuals who are proficient in the classroom
but incompetent in day-to-day living. If these are the most
significant things about your characters, however, then
they are not going to seem much more than cardboard cut-
outs, and no one is going to get very excited about them,
including you. The argument that there are such people in

real life overlooks the fact that real-life people are more complex than they appear at first glance.

Let's say you want to write a novel about a long-distance trucker. You have a vague plot in mind about his truck breaking down in the desert, even of his being hijacked. But all you really know at this point is that truckers fascinate you, and your mind is playing around with the idea of basing a novel on such a person.

Ask a few people how they envision a long-distance truck driver, and you may wind up with the following composite: a burly loner who never finished high school, who gets his kicks out of terrorizing little cars on freeways and using gutter language on his CB radio.

There are, undoubtedly, some truckers who fit this description. But there are also long-distance truckers who are college-educated and can't get jobs in their chosen fields. Or they need to make some money before they take on a less lucrative job. There are professional drivers who choose this occupation and are good at it, and truckers whose spouses go along on their cross-country trips and help with the driving. Even if your character conforms to many of the stereotypes the public has of a particular occupation or economic group, make sure that in some noticeable way *your* trucker is different. This will make him far more real to your audience.

Is it a good idea to pattern fictional characters after people we know? While such an approach may seem expedient—getting a character ready-made—it's hardly worth the price. You must change so many things about this person anyway to avoid a possible lawsuit that you might just as well invent the character from scratch. This does not mean that you can't borrow a mannerism from one person, an occupation from another, a facial feature from a third, etc. Writers do this all the time. But if you are consciously thinking of one particular person each time you have your character appear on the page, you run the risk of having the real-life person—rather than the character you need for your novel—dictate what your fictional person will or won't do.

If, for example, you are secretly portraying the young wife of your next-door neighbor, and you know her to be fairly straitlaced, you may have considerable trouble getting her to run off with another man in your story. That such a woman might do just such a thing is beside the point. You will have better luck if you choose a few of her characteristics that fascinate you and endow the character you created with them. Otherwise you may find that the dialogue and motivation of your ready-made character just don't ring true. Instead of speaking as your character should speak, she will sound too much like your neighbor's wife, and be unconvincing.

The names you choose for your characters are also important. You do not want a name that calls too much attention to itself or it will detract from the story; you don't want a name that jars, however slightly, every time it appears on the page, unless that is your intent. Heroines do not have to have musical names such as Roxanne, Stephanie, Tiffany, or Michelle. By the same token, avoid such model-perfect names as Darien and Sean for your men. It is especially important to avoid names that are too similar to one another. You don't want to confuse your reader for a moment. You want him to read the book with a finger ready to turn the next page the second his eyes reach the last line. Don't name one character Doris, and another Dorothy or Delores and risk the reader's having to thumb back to the first chapter to figure out who is who.

In choosing names, it is easy to fall back on stereotypes. You should research the names of characters carefully, according to their ages, the region of the country where they live, and their nationality, but avoid naming them exactly what your reader would expect. While it is true that in certain parts of the country men may be called more often by nicknames than by their given names, and women may traditionally have two first names, you would not, if you were setting your story in South Carolina, want to call your protagonist Billy Bob and his wife Ellen Sue, since this would reinforce the stereotype. Even if you come from a small town in Georgia where you know for a fact that almost every woman has a two-syllable first name and a one-syllable middle name, reverse the pattern for a character or two. Make one of your characters stand out simply by naming her Betty, and another Jo Alice, not Alice Jo.

There are exceptions to such guidelines, of course—to everything that is said in this book, most certainly—and sometimes the exception is so beautifully and artfully done that it becomes the perfect choice. But do keep your characters' ages in mind when you write. Someday there may be a lot of grandmothers named Lisa and Kim, but not right now.

Liking a character

Another question often asked of writers is whether or not the main character need be likable—if not at the beginning, at least by the end of the novel. Of course not. Our long-distance trucker may be truly abominable and still worth writing about. What is needed to hold your readers' interest is not love of the main character—though the writer's task is much easier if this is the case—but an attraction to him, even a perverse one. Empathy, perhaps. Readers must believe that such a character could and would exist and act in a certain way, whether they like him or not.

Readers may stick with a novel not because they love the

protagonist but because his very stubbornness—or even his evilness—fascinates them. They will wonder how he ever got to be the way he is and what on earth he will do next. They will care what happens to him out of curiosity, if not sympathy, and will keep reading to see if he gets his just deserts.

If you want readers to love your central character, you must see to it that he or she has faults, not necessarily huge or glaring ones, but enough faults to make readers feel the protagonist is a real person, not a paragon. A loving parent must, at times, speak harshly and be unjust. A mature husband must have some annoying habit or worry or weakness that makes him real. If he is too marvelous, then liking him (or disliking him!) is too easy. Readers don't feel challenged and are therefore likely to be bored.

On the other hand, writers may play up the hero's faults too much, assuming that the virtues already show through. They are aghast when the editor remarks that the protagonist seems stingy or cruel.

Early in your novel, give the readers some hint as to the nature of your character: the way he answers his wife; the concern he shows his son; the harsh way he speaks to the cleaning woman; even the way he treats his dog. Don't tell your readers what he is like; show them. Not everything, either. Just enough. There have to be some surprises left so the ending of your story is not too predictable.

Knowing your characters

"Writers are crazy," says novelist Elizabeth Spencer. "I've made all these people up, and then I think I've got to spend time getting to know them."

She's right, of course. And if we knew our characters thoroughly before we began working on a novel, the writing would be far easier. But often we find that no matter how well we think out a character beforehand, it is mostly in the actual writing that he reveals himself to us. This is not unlike a real-life situation, in which we may have heard a great deal about a guest that we will be meeting at dinner, but until we have talked with her and seen her interacting with others, we have only a superficial knowledge of what she is like.

In the planning stage of your novel, it's helpful to write profiles of your main characters as well as a summary of your plot. Write as much as you know or feel about a character—age, educational background, relationship with parents, with spouse, with children, with siblings. . . . How does he spend his spare time? What would he most like to accomplish? Is he a bit of a snob or is he self-effacing? Does he contribute to causes? What does he think about philosophically? What kind of music does he like? Is he an organized person? A slob? Does he plan his life or just fall into it, more or less?

You may write only a page about a character, or you may find that one idea leads to the next and you are writing seven, eight, nine pages about this one person, most of which may never turn up in your novel. It is the same as researching a facet of any book—the history of the region, for example. You may use only a fraction of the research in the story, but your knowledge of where this man went to school will help you shape the way he talks, the people he associates with, and all the other aspects of his personality.

Breathing life into your characters

Toni Morrison has said of this task: "Anyone can think up a story. But trying to breathe life into characters, allow them space, make them people whom I care about is hard. I have only twenty-six letters of the alphabet; I don't have color or music. I must use my craft to make the reader see the colors and hear the sounds."

Some writers go into minute descriptions—the droop of the eyelids, the sag of the mouth at the corners, the age spots on the hands, and so forth. They are so good at descriptive phrases that they can paint a portrait with words.

But the physical description of the character alone will not bring him to life. Neither will his name. Readers need to hear how he *sounds* when he talks, to see how his body moves when he walks, how he relates to the members of his family.

If we choose, we can accomplish a great deal without saying what a character looks like at all, concentrating more on his feelings, his actions and mannerisms. There are authors who believe that the more they leave to the reader's imagination visually, the more the reader can identify with the protagonist.

You should make sure that the details you choose to tell about the character are the important things—the qualities or characteristics that help define this person, that are clues to his personality and the kind of life he has lived. A few specifics about his looks and a habit or two may be all readers need to form a mental picture, and they will fill in the rest as they get to know the man, watching him move in and out of the scenes.

It's not easy keeping a character alive and real throughout the entire 300 or so pages of a novel. While you may be excused for feeling that if you can bring two or three of the central figures of your story into focus, you should be able to slide by with the others, you can't be excused if you actually do only that. A teacher with thirty-nine children in her classroom may not relish still another, but somehow she's got to care for him. The same is true of characters in a novel.

Actress Meryl Streep was asked about her unusual ability to create radically different characters on screen. "It probably has to do with my world view, which is that everybody's different, but they're all the same in some way," she answered. "I just like to investigate all these different people to see what the commonality is with me. When I start with the script and I read their story, I hear the 'Ping!' that makes a connection with my own life or experience. But it's also the thing that makes me see where all these different people link up."

You should not describe every doorman, every stranger, every clerk, every police officer in your story, just because he or she happens to make a cameo appearance. When you go to the trouble of informing readers in detail what a character looks like or thinks or says or does, then they have every right to expect that this person is going to be important somehow in the novel. If you give equal attention to everyone who drifts in and out of the pages, it will only confuse your readers and detract from the people who are the main focus of your story.

But if, for example, you have one protagonist, two supporting characters, and three more who are fairly important to the plot, plus a whole cast of extras, readers will want to know the protagonist inside and out, the two supporting characters almost as well, and also a great deal about the three others who are important to the story.

The writer does this by mentally *becoming* these people during the writing. Even the bitchy ones, the ugly ones, the evil ones, the horrible, complaining, whining ones.

Becoming a horrible person

While you may be writing about a despicable person from the point of view of the central character who has every right to dislike him, you as the author must know far more about this horrible person than the protagonist does—at this point in the story, anyway. If you are writing from the main character's point of view, you may not reveal anything that the protagonist himself has not yet discovered about the H.P. (Horrible Person). On the other hand, you may give the reader little insights into the feelings of the H.P. simply by describing the way he holds his hands as he says a particular phrase, the slump of his shoulders, the tapping of his foot, so that while readers are seeing nothing more than what the leading character could have seen if he weren't so upset, they may deduce something more, something that the protagonist, in all his fury, may have been too distracted to notice.

You can best accomplish this not only by describing the H.P. as the main character sees him, but by trying to imagine yourself in the H.P.'s place—feeling what he is feeling, wearing what he is wearing, and speaking from the H.P.'s own lips, from the H.P.'s own experience. *This* will bring the character to life. Here is an example:

Frank stood at Wally's desk with the report in his hands. He gripped the papers so hard that he felt the pressure of his own fingers against his thumb.

"I thought I had done exactly what you asked," he said, his words coming out in hard little icy bits of control.

Wally shifted slightly in his chair, but his calm smile never wavered.

"Exactly what I asked, but no more. I expected better from you, Frank."

"I'm a mind reader? I'm supposed to know what else you want when you haven't even told me?"

Everything about Wally's office was too perfect—the neat stacks of tax materials arranged just so on top of the file cabinets; the desk top, with its matching accessories, in one straight row along the back. Wally himself was meticulously arranged—his nails squarely trimmed, his hair politely combed, the perfect suit, the matching tie—nothing out of step, everything squeezed into some preordained concept of perfection.

"When you reach a certain level in our corporation, Frank,

we expect creativity, that's all." Now the perfectly manicured fingers of one hand were massaging the other, as though rubbing life back into something long frozen, as if the only way to inject feeling into a vice-president of the Mercott Corporation was through a sort of auto-resuscitation.

Frank's anger surged again.

The readers may not like Wally, the H.P. in this instance, any better after reading the above, but they at least know he has problems; they at least know that his perfectly ordered life has its drawbacks, and that underneath that calm exterior, there is tension trying to work its way out. The readers see this, but whether Frank makes the connection or not, we don't know—he's too angry.

This does not mean that you have changed point of view. You do not suddenly switch and tell the story from the viewpoint of the Horrible Person. But knowing him as well as you must, you may select what to show the reader about him.

If, as the novelist, I become a fifty-two-year-old man whose wife has walked out on him and I'm furious about it, how am I going to act toward the waitress who serves my coffee? If she makes the same kind of mindless remarks that my wife used to make, if she has the same habit of not finishing her sentences, if there is anything about her at all that I can attack—from the sour smell of her breath to the ketchup on her apron—I'll probably say something sarcastic and feel I have every right to.

Never mind that this is unfair. Never mind that I am projecting my wife's failings onto the waitress. Never mind that I may richly deserve to be walked out on. To describe this man sitting at this table in the diner, I as the author must become him, feel what he is feeling in his own distorted way, even though, at the same time, I still am describing it all through the eyes of the central character. The

protagonist and the reader may see the same things, yet—
if the writing is skillful—something that provokes fury in
the protagonist may evoke sympathy in the reader, and the
reader will understand both.

But then too, I must become the waitress. When it's her
turn to speak, I must no longer see her as the H.P. sees her,
but I must stand there in the soiled apron that I had washed
and pressed only the night before, conscious that I'm not
the most attractive person on earth. But here I am, a
decent hard-working woman, and this disagreeable man is
speaking to me in such a cutting way. How will I respond?
What kind of look crosses my face? What am I feeling, and
how much do I dare say?

The author can become all these people, the horrible as
well as the wonderful, because he too has moments of
arrogance, of cowardice, of being mean-spirited as well as
sadistic. And by tapping that vein within ourselves, however shameful, however hidden, we may expand upon it,
dwell upon it, magnify it there on paper until it is *our*
meanness, *our* arrogance, *our* selfishness that we are writing about, and we are drawing from our own experience.

Of course, no one else need know just how much of
ourselves we are exposing. Often not even writers realize
the degree to which their writing is autobiographical. But
we are able to do this—we take this risk—because we
accept the fact that everything we have ever felt or seen or
heard or experienced, no matter how marvelous or disgust-
ing or terrifying or brave, someone else has experienced,
too. And we can therefore trust the generosity of our readers when we put our thoughts and feelings down on paper.

🎕 6

Merging Character and Plot

EDITORS LOOK FOR NOVELS that have believable, distinctive characters in a situation that holds their interest and leads them on. They know that if you have a great plot but cardboard characters, readers will find it difficult to empathize with them. If, on the other hand, you have characters so real that you can see their faces and hear their voices, but no plot worth writing about, it's as if they were all dressed up with no place to go. "So?" the reader keeps asking, "What's the point?"

Establishing boundaries

When you know your characters well enough, however, they can help you construct the story. The conflict and the plot will have natural boundaries, determined by where these people live, their occupations, their educational backgrounds, and their psychological make-up. Knowing all these things about your character will suggest situations and problems to you that they might face, how they might deal with them, and what the outcome might be.

So, too, if you have an exciting situation—you know what the major theme and plot will be before any characters come to mind—then there are limits as to whom you may invite into your story. Each additional element you add during the planning establishes boundaries. With a certain location in mind, for instance, you know who would most likely live there, what their interests would be, and how they make their living. So your characters come more into focus. If it's to be a spy story, you can be fairly sure that your protagonist is a risk-taker.

To use the novel about the long-distance trucker as an example: You have the situation and plot firmly in mind but have not yet filled out the personality of your main character. You at least know his occupation, and starting with that, you may know a good deal more about him than you think. Assuming, that is, that you know anything about truckers. If you don't, you need to do considerably more research before you begin writing your novel.

In writing profiles of your main characters, subplots will pop out at every turn. The more you know about your characters, the more possibilities you are going to see for conflict—between the conservative uncle and his free-thinking niece, between the cop and the religious demonstrators. When you begin a scene, you will know instinctively whether your hero would enter a singles bar or buy a lottery ticket or attend a ballet, and if he would not, you will change your game plan accordingly.

Avoiding the expected

Take the long-distance trucker. You know, let's say, that you want him big; you want him burly. You don't want him college-educated, and maybe you don't even want him married. A loner. But mindful of the stereotype you may be creating, you decide to change at least one thing about him that readers would not expect: Instead of making him foul-mouthed, this man is a Bible-reading, soft-spoken loner who feels that the world is going lickety-split to hell. Instead of listening to rock stations on his cross-country trips, he tunes in the religious programs instead. He listens to the revival preachers and the Sunday services and the Gospel Hour.

This one change from the stereotype in your main character immediately suggests a number of plots or subplots. What if: (a) On a lonely night when he is feeling especially vulnerable, he is propositioned by one of the hookers who work the truck stops? (b) He picks up a young, scared female hitchhiker who is running away from home? (c) He comes across a member of Hell's Angels whose motorcycle has broken down, and the man needs a lift to the nearest garage? The possibilities go on and on. What if he picks up a Bible-quoting traveling preacher and decides he can't stand him?

At this point, when the writer finds himself excited by an unexpected idea, he must be careful not to do the obvious.

What is the reader most likely to expect if the Bible-reading truck driver is propositioned by a hooker on a lonely night? That he would give in, probably, and discover he isn't as righteous as he thought. So what if the author has the trucker take her into his room, but spend the whole night preaching to her about her life style? What might the reader expect next? That he would convert her? Maybe. That she would seduce him? Possibly. So what if she leaves, thinking "What a jerk!" and after he is fifty miles down the road, *she* has second thoughts and wants to catch up with him?

In the earlier example about Jane, a perfectionistic young woman advertising for a roommate, probably 99% of your readers would expect the roommate to turn out to be a slob, that this is where the conflict would come in. So don't write it that way. Make the roommate even more meticulous and precise than Jane is. It's helpful, sometimes, when you are thinking out a plot, to keep asking yourself, "What would the reader most naturally expect?" and then make sure your character does something else.

Plotting, of course, involves much more than simply deciding what your readers anticipate and then taking a different path. Sometimes the plot *does* turn out the way readers expect, but then unforeseen things must happen along the way to provide the suspense.

If Bernie King, owner of a jewelry store in a crime-infested area, always takes his earnings to the bank at noon on Fridays, we just know he is going to be robbed. If, however, Bernie has elaborate methods for outwitting a potential mugger—he disguises himself, he carries the money in a paper sack part of the time and other times he carries it under his shirt—and if there is another problem in the story that captures more of our interest than this, then we will be taken off guard when a robbery happens, or at least we will be interested in *how* it could happen after all of these precautions.

When writing the unexpected, be sure to make it convincing, natural. Novels and stories about a self-righteous person giving in to sins of the flesh have been written many times before. In Somerset Maugham's story, "Rain" (originally titled "Miss Thompson"), a repressed missionary almost succeeds in converting a young prostitute, but—when they succumb to lust—she reverts to her former ways. So how will your story about the trucker be different? What is the original spark that comes solely from you, that makes it the story only you could write?

Motivation

A common mistake that many novelists make is to force a character to do something at the outset of the story because it is necessary for what will happen later. It may not be entirely convincing, for example, that a protagonist would go to Denver at Christmas without his wife in chapter four, but if he doesn't, he will never meet Cynthia in chapter six, and therefore what happens in chapter seven could never occur. So the author sends Bill to Denver on Christmas Eve. That takes care of the author's motivation, but what about Bill's?

Motivation is a chief stumbling block in writing a novel, and one the beginning writer often overlooks. He is so relieved to have thought of a theme and a plot and a character and an ending, that he does not stop to ask himself some elementary questions. If, he concludes, Bob and Delores have an affair, and Delores tells her sister, and her sister gets drunk at a party and blabs the secret, everything will come out at the end as planned. But *would* his two main characters have an affair? And if this is convincing, would Delores actually tell her sister? Does she confide in others so easily? And if the author is finally satisfied that Delores would tell, would her sister really get drunk at a party and let the secret out of the bag, or would she be likely to do something much different?

In plot after plot, motivation may turn out to be the stickler. A character's odd behavior must be explained—if not now, later; if not spelled out word for word, then enough must be implied so readers can figure it out for themselves.

If a novel begins, "Ellen's mother hated men," readers eventually have to know why.

If a man goes to the mountains to live by himself for a year, readers need to know what prompted that action. It isn't enough just to say he wanted to get away for a while or to be by himself. When he comes back into the picture again, readers will want to know what he has been doing all this time and how he has changed.

If "Beverly Ingstrom was never her father's favorite," readers want to know why. You should not have to say in a covering letter to your editor what should be evident in the manuscript itself. You cannot accompany every copy of your novel sold to explain what isn't there.

Confronting the question

Another mistake, easy to make, is the failure to take into account obvious questions or events that would bring matters to a head. Let's say the author keeps the story going by having the telephone ring so the protagonist doesn't have to answer his wife's question; or the secretary walks in just as the boss is about to open the drawer and discover the cash box is missing.

Such devices are too coincidental, even though they *could* happen. The fact that they did in this story, in exactly the right place, makes us feel that the author is getting off too easily.

How much more interesting it would be to *let* the husband answer the question. *Let* the boss discover that the cash box is missing. Now what? Introduce a new angle into your plot. What will the husband do then? Follow up one lie with another, increasing the tension? What will the secretary do? Let the boss make his discovery, then fake astonishment? Sometimes a plot can be improved just by the refusal to sidestep the obvious.

In my novel *The Keeper*, Jacob Karpinski quits his job without explanation, and becomes suspicious and secretive. Mrs. Karpinski, out of pride, tells no one, hoping that in time it will all blow over. But she and her teen-age son do not yet know that Jacob is mentally ill, and when Nick confronts his father, Jacob tells him that he left his job because the Communists are after him—that all the men at work are in on it:

> Nick tried to understand. "You're *serious?* The whole Life Trust Company?"

"Shhh." Jacob put one hand on Nick's wrist. "Don't tell your mother."

Uncertainty grabbed at Nick again, dissolving the faith he had felt only seconds before. "She's got to know, Dad."

"She won't believe me." Jacob's eyes were changing again. "No one believes me. You don't believe me yourself. You believe Edmunds."

Nick shook his head, bewildered. "Dad, I just don't know what to think."

"Listen." The fingers gripped his wrist so tightly that Nick could feel Jacob's nails digging into the flesh. "They've got spies all over. They train them there—then send them out."

"You've been with Life Trust for three years, Dad. You just find this out?"

Jacob ignored the question. "Everywhere you look, they've got spies."

If the conversation had ended there, I would have been avoiding the obvious next question: Why doesn't Jacob do something about it? Why doesn't he go to the police?

This is only chapter two, however, and if Jacob went to the police now and told them that an entire insurance company in Chicago was a front for Communist activity, the police would have ordered a psychiatric evaluation. End of story. Instead, Nick asks the crucial question, and in answering, Jacob gives us an even better understanding of paranoid schizophrenia:

"Why don't you go to the police?"

"Ha!" Jacob withdrew his hand. "The police are in on it too."

Nick's back felt cold, as though a shadow were moving across the room. "The whole Chicago police force?"

Jacob gave no answer, and the coldness settled in Nick's chest.

"Go to the FBI, then."

The smile played on Jacob's lips again: "They've infiltrated the FBI too."

When Nick spoke again, he hardly recognized his own voice. The color had gone out of the words; his voice was flat: "What are you going to do, Dad? We going to move or what? You going to get another job?"

He watched as his father hunched over his knees again, large hands dangling, his face drawn. "Only way I'm going to leave Chicago is in a box. *They'll* see to that."

A wave of panic swept over Nick. On the outside he was the same Nick Karpinski, but he was leading a double life. They were both living double lives, he and his father.

Moving characters in and out of the pages

While plot and characters do reinforce each other, it's not entirely true that if you know your characters well enough, they will take the lead. Somebody's got to be the tour guide. Authors tell their characters, in essence, where they are going to go, but let them have some say as to how they will get there. And writers are often surprised at the detours characters take and the passengers they pick up along the way.

In *The Keeper*, Jacob Karpinski, being paranoid schizophrenic, quite naturally led me from one bizarre episode to the next. What he had done in a previous scene, what had been said to him, and how he interacted with his wife all helped dictate just what the next scene would be.

I knew, when I began the novel, that at some point Jacob was going to disassemble the inner workings of the toilet tank looking for hidden microphones. I knew, too, that he was going to do something that would upset his son very much, but I didn't know just what that would be.

When Nick comes home after a day out with friends, having taken silly pictures of each other for the yearbook, he feels that at last he is accepted in this school. I realized that Jacob, unknowingly, must do something to jar Nick's newfound self-esteem. Suspicious about where his son has been, whom he has seen, and indeed, whether even Nick might be spying on him, Jacob steals into Nick's room that night, takes the undeveloped film from Nick's camera, and submerges it under three inches of water in the bathtub.

This was a surprise to me, not that he took the film and ruined it, but that he put it under water. Why under water? Why the bathtub? Because it didn't make sense. Because much of what Jacob does makes no sense, and this is one of the most frightening things about living with someone who is mentally ill.

In writing your novel, you will not want so many characters in the book that there is a jumble of backgrounds and problems, yet you need enough to give the scenes variety and keep the plot running smoothly. It is not at all unusual for a novel to be completed before the author or editor decides that a certain character is dispensable—that his few good lines could be given to someone else—or that he could easily be merged with another character of no great importance.

Nor is it unusual for a book to be written and then a character added during the revision. The author may discover that the protagonist needs a close friend in whom he can confide, so that readers will have a window on the main character's thoughts without the necessity of long pages of soliloquy.

Characters who are important to the story should either make regular appearances, or their names should be mentioned enough to keep them firmly in the reader's memory. If Mrs. Marlow is mentioned in chapter one, for example, and not again for the next eleven chapters, readers may quite naturally assume that the poor woman is wasting away, and that she is certainly not of great value to the plot.

The juggling of characters—knowing it's time to bring

Mrs. Marlow to the fore again—helps influence plot. We don't bring her to life just to convince the readers she is still hanging in there; her appearance must add to the story. Every character, every scene, every dialogue, every sentence must move the plot along. Readers do not need to know that Mrs. Marlow wears French lingerie unless this helps define her personality. We do not have to know anything at all about Mrs. Marlow unless she is more important to the story than a bank teller with whom the protagonist makes a transaction. If she has a place in the novel, that must be because it wouldn't be complete without her, not just because the author decided he needed another female character.

The wonderful thing about writing is that—compared to painting with watercolors, for example—we can revise and repair with relative ease. We can move paragraphs about and delete and add until we have at last brought our characters and plot into harmony with each other. It is this re-thinking of a novel—this pondering and probing—that uses an author's mind at full capacity. It's hard work, but if writers are not willing to go over a manuscript page by page, paragraph by paragraph, then line by line, and finally word by word, they are in the wrong profession.

For Toni Morrison, there's no question. Talking of all the work that writing entails, she says: "It's not always a pleasure, sometimes I don't enjoy it, sometimes I can't even do it—but it's the place where I live, where I really am. It's home."

The different drafts of a novel

Before word processors came into vogue, it was easier to talk about the separate drafts of a novel because you could count them. There are still authors who write a novel numerous times in longhand before putting it on a disk. But whether the book is written in longhand or on the type-writer or word processor, whether each chapter is rewritten before going on to the next, or whether the whole novel is written at once, many writers would say that the first draft is the hardest. Author Herman Wouk described writing as the "difficult process of gritting one's teeth and putting down one word after another," while Oscar Wilde said that he spent his mornings putting the comma in and his afternoons taking the comma out.

The first draft is the bare framework on which everything hangs. At this point you, as author, are moving characters about from scene to scene, much like the director of a play at the first rehearsal. Nobody moves very elegantly; the characters seem self-conscious about where they are to go, and they read their lines awkwardly. You are setting the stage for the rest of the novel. You are getting a sense of your own style, your own voice; for the first time your characters have appeared in front of the footlights, and you are getting to know them.

Whenever you think of the "perfect" way to say something, of course, you will put it down on paper. You certainly don't want to forget it between the first and second drafts. But you're not aiming for perfection. Not yet. Not nearly yet. I have known writers who would rather go outside naked to fetch the newspaper than risk letting anyone look at a first draft.

The second draft is a more relaxing venture. The groundwork has already been laid; you don't have to think it all out for the first time. And because you know that many more drafts lie ahead, you can, at your leisure, flesh out your scenes as ideas come to you, not worring about whether they are "right," just playing with your characters, getting a feel for the action, adding richness and depth. And again, like actors on stage, the characters themselves seem more comfortable; their lines read with more expression.

In the third draft, it's back to business again. By now, you will plan to make certain scenes stand out. You'll take more time with every paragraph, every chapter, trying to get the most you can from every sentence. Though each word does not have to be the final choice in this run-through, you had better be getting close to what it is you wanted to do in your novel. And while there may be flat scenes or patches of dialogue here and there that need polishing, for the most part you will want your third draft to read well, with good writing on every page.

An earlier chapter discussed the advantages of revising each section before going on to the next one. In thinking about the separate drafts of the entire novel, it is easier to see why this is helpful.

In the first draft of the first chapter, let's say, your leading character may walk into the diner, hang up his jacket, and order the swiss steak. In the second draft of the first chapter, he may take off his jacket, stuff it in one corner of the booth, and order the blue-plate special. In the third draft, you may decide to have him stand inside the door of the diner in his muddy boots and torn jacket and order a cheeseburger to go. He is still Clyde Bellows, and he is still a construction worker, but with each draft you are getting a little closer to his personality, his mannerisms, the things that make him real.

If you hastily type out the entire novel about Clyde Bellows without getting to know him as well as you should, if you allow him to take off his jacket, hang it up, and order the swiss steak, and it is not until the second revision of the entire novel that you discover that the man is really quite shy, that he feels awkward eating inside where people might look at him, then you will have scene after scene to revise and change, chapter after chapter.

If you had stayed with the first scene until you decided that no, Clyde Bellows would be the type to order a lunch to go and eat it outside alone somewhere, then you have made it that much easier on yourself in the chapters to come. If, when you read what you have written the day before, you are astounded at your own cleverness, delight in your own dialogue, and laugh at your own humor, then you are far more likely to begin the next chapter with exhilaration and hope.

But not every writer works this way. Some writers claim just the opposite: it is only in writing about a character that they get to know him. They say that they can write just as well and as fast by laying out the whole thing in rough form and then revising eleven times, if necessary. They insist that motivation, for them, is seeing the whole thing done, no matter how many times they might have to rewrite it.

How many more drafts there are between the third and the final one is up to you. It is possible to wind the novel up fairly quickly. It is also possible to rewrite so many times you lose count. Speaking of his novel *Riddley Walker*, which took five and a half years to write, Russell Hoban says: "I had to go back to page one 14 times to get the effect I wanted. There were too many characters. There was too much action. With each revision, the story became more concentrated."

More often than not, you will rewrite certain paragraphs or pages many more times than the rest of the manuscript. The first and the last drafts are frequently the most difficult—the first because you are doing everything for the first time, the last because it's your final chance to polish and catch mistakes before your editor sees the manuscript.

In a good novel, authors know, the plot, the situations,

the characters, the dialogue all move along in harmony with the main theme—exploring it, magnifying it, expanding on it, bringing both conflicts and characters into focus, all building toward a climax and a final resolution. And the thought that all of this should be evident in the final draft of the manuscript is one that gives even the best of writers pause.

"Every book is a problem," says Philip Roth. "You set the terms of the problem crudely in the first six months, and then you spend the next eighteen months or three years saying, 'Can I solve this problem?'"

But for those who might consider the whole process so forbidding that they are loath to begin, author Maya Angelou advises simply setting aside a time and saying, "If it comes, good; if it doesn't come, good; I'll just sit here."

♔ 7

Point of View

WILL YOU USE FIRST-PERSON singular for your novel, with the story narrated by the main character? Will you keep the point of view of the protagonist, but write in third person? Will you alternate between characters, writing one chapter or section from one character's point of view and another section or chapter as seen through another character's eyes? Or will you, as the author, be omniscient, knowing the minds of all the characters at once and sharing with your reader how each is feeling and what he is thinking? Each choice has advantages and limitations.

One way to approach these questions is to write the first page from the omniscient viewpoint, then rewrite it in first person, then try third person, deciding which voice feels most natural, lends itself most easily to the story.

First-person singular

When the "I" character tells the story in his own words, the entire novel will have to be written from his point of view, however distorted or sentimental or cynical this may be. As he changes within the novel, of course, his voice will change to reflect what is going on in his head and heart. But if you know this character thoroughly, you will get into his rhythm of speech, his thought processes, his philosophy of life. Eudora Welty does this well in "Why I Live at the P.O.," in which the action is related by "Sister," a young woman having a quarrel with her relatives. By the end of this short story, readers know what Sister thinks of everyone else in her family and what they, in turn, think of her. Will your main character speak in short sentences? Will he be given to long philosophical musings? As he grows on you and comes alive on the page, you become this person in your imagination and are able to anticipate what he will do or say next, and exactly how he will say it.

First-person singular is often a good vehicle for humor, particularly the self-deprecating kind. Everyone loves to laugh—especially at somebody else. And when a character induces the reader to laugh at him, the reader is happy to oblige.

The trick in a first-person-singular novel is to allow readers to see flaws in a character that he may not be able to see himself. Yet if he is telling the story, how can he not be aware of them? The author can achieve this by having the narrator pass over something he has said so casually that the readers can tell he doesn't see the significance of it; they, however, do.

The following is the opening scene from my novel *The Year of the Gopher*, about a 17-year-old boy whose parents are pushing him toward an Ivy League school. It is told in first person by George Richards:

> At twelve, the sun reached the *Touch of Silk* calendar on my wall; it shone on the legs of the girl in the picture as though she were tanning only half her body. By twelve thirty-three it had touched the tip of my boomerang, and five minutes later it was fading the photo of Karen Gunderson. There were thumbtack holes in Karen Gunderson's picture where I'd decided, once, to give her acne. Karen Gunderson never had a pimple in her life.
> I scratched my stomach and let one foot hang over the edge

of the mattress. If Mom didn't yell pretty soon, I was going to waste the whole day. The window was open, and the dry yellow leaves of the box elder scraped against the screen. I could hear a portable radio on the steps outside, then the postman wrestling with the mail slot.

Kerplunk. Downstairs, something hit the slate floor of the foyer.

Dartmouth, I told myself.

Kerplunk again.

Princeton. I rolled over and tunneled beneath the pillow. Those were the only two catalogs yet to come.

"George!" Mom called. "You just got Princeton and Dartmouth. Get up, or you'll waste the whole day."

The reader will smile when George says that if his mom doesn't yell pretty soon, he'll waste the whole day. In this 17-year-old's half-sleep, it makes perfect sense, but the reader can also see the immaturity of a young man putting the responsibility on his mother to get him up and going.

First-person singular may also be a good choice if there is something about the way your character speaks that would help the story ring true, that might give it more local flavor. In *Unexpected Pleasures*, April Ruth Bates is a 16-year-old high school dropout whose two older sisters have turned to prostitution. When a group of women, the local "decency committee," comes to call, April's next older sister, Thomasine, throws a coat over her slip and high-tails it out the back door of the trailer, leaving April to fend for herself:

"Haven't done *nothin'*!" I said aloud, and I didn't know how mad I was till I heard my own voice.

"We didn't say you had, dear." Mrs. Dawson kept on squeezing my arm. "But when a home is obviously a bad influence on a child, the only thing to do is find a better place for that child to live."

I felt just like somebody had punched me square in the stomach. I wanted to yell for Thomasine, but I knew she was sitting back in the woods in our daddy's coat and wouldn't come out for anything in this world. Daddy hadn't been home the night before, and wherever he was, he wasn't in no shape to help me. Neither was Dorothy. I'd been left to myself for most of my sixteen years, but I never felt so alone as I did right then.

"You don't got the right," I says in this little bitty voice that hardly had any breath to it.

"My dear, I'm not threatening you, but believe me, I have friends in the courthouse, and I will do whatever it takes to get you removed from this place," Mrs. Dawson tells me.

"Like where?" I says, almost a whisper.

She looks straight into my eyes. "We're considering a number of possibilities, and to be honest, the juvenile home is one of them."

I sprung up off my chair like it was hot and leaped around behind it, keeping the chair between me and the ladies.

"I'm not going to the juvenile home!" I says. "I ain't done *nothin'*!"

Mrs. Dawson sighed and exchanged looks with the other women.

"Of course, the *ideal* arrangement would be a kind family that would take you in," said the woman who looked like a sparrow, and the other women nodded, "but truth to tell, April, we just can't find one that will have you—because of your sisters, you see."

A great big lump worked its way up my throat. Felt like a baseball. Seemed to me I was growing smaller and smaller till finally I was just this little speck behind the chair and the women was all looking down at me like hens about to scratch. They had me, I knew. I tried to think of one single, solitary person I could ask to help me. The men at the Amoco station were nice, but they wasn't about to take me home. And Tillie, at the Laundromat, was okay, but I think she'd had a crazy spell sometime in her life and I didn't want to get mixed up with that. I felt my chin start to tremble and I pressed my teeth together hard to keep from crying.

And then Sister Perry's face lights up like a Coca-Cola sign, and she says, "But we've got good news for you, April Ruth, if *you're* willing."

I felt like I was hanging suspended and the committee had hold of the ropes.

The women were smiling at each other. "It's quite romantic, really," says Mrs. Dawson, and she gives a little giggle. "Somebody wants to marry you."

I could feel my teeth pulling away from each other as my jaw dropped. Buddy Travis, from typing, I thought.

"Somebody who has watched you grow up and wants to give you a home," added Mrs. Perry.

"And take care of you," said the sparrow.

I looked quickly from one woman to the other. I tried to think of the mechanic's name at the Amoco station. Was it him?

"Foster Williams," said Mrs. Dawson.

I come back around the chair and sat down on it hard. Just couldn't get it through my head. Foster! The bridgeman! And before I could say anything, the women all starts in again, about how he's lonely and he's a good hardworking man, got this house all to hisself, don't drink much to speak of, and he'd be good to me. They used the kinds of voices that have violins playing in the background, and everyone of 'em made it sound like if Foster Williams had asked for them instead of me, they would've left their husbands and run right off.

If you have a good ear for the way people talk, your writing may fall very easily into first person. One thing to consider, however, is that when a character is telling the story himself, you cannot have any scenes taking place behind his back, anything happening he does not know about. He can hear about them later, of course, and he can talk about things someone else told him, but when you choose first person, you get up with your main character in the morning and go to bed with him at night. You are with him constantly. You cannot leave this person's side even for a moment, for you must "become" this character for the duration of the novel.

Any character who tells his story from the first-person singular point of view is likely to get reader sympathy, because the readers are allowed into his thoughts and feelings. Readers may not approve of or condone what he does, but they will understand why he does it. Writing from the villain's viewpoint, therefore, allows the writer to bring originality into a novel, to introduce ambiguity, to write a book that will be argued about and discussed.

Third-person narrative

You are also glued to your main character if you choose to see the entire novel from his point of view rather than from the omniscient point of view. But in using third-person narrative, you, the author, not the character, are doing the telling, as though you are accompanying this one person around, recording and then relating everything he does or says, including the thoughts and feelings he confides in you, never entering a room or a scene unless he does. While you may record what some other character is doing, it is always through the eyes and ears and thoughts of this one person you are with.

In other words, if Janice is the main character, you should not say, *Hal, disappointed, sat down in the chair,* because Janice cannot know how he feels. She may surmise how he feels, however, so you may say, *Hal sat down in the chair, and his shoulders slumped. "Disappointed?" Janice asked.* You can report what Janice observes or thinks, but not what another character feels except as it *appears* to Janice.

You may choose third-person narrative for a variety of

reasons. Perhaps you don't feel comfortable trying to sustain what essentially amounts to a long monologue for the entire length of a novel. Or you may want to make some observations that the main character himself would hardly put into words. Consider this excerpt from my novel *Revelations*:

> During the last fourteen years, however, Mary had felt less and less special. When people stared at her chalk-white face in the department stores, she was not certain it was out of respect. When the girls who went braless in hot pants had been married off before anyone else, and Mary stayed home with her rheumatoid mother, she did not feel that she was the envy of anybody. And when on her few chaste dates with Marbury's eligible bachelors, she compared the subjects they discussed with the ones on the cover of *Redbook* and *Cosmopolitan*, she wondered if "The Myth of the Mutual Orgasm" was something she would ever be able to talk about, or whether it was still light years away.

You may choose the third-person narrative style because it allows you, if you wish, to maintain a certain distance from your main character. If a protagonist is outgoing and the very sort to tell the readers what he's feeling, first person may work very well; but if he is guarded about what he has to say and never wears his heart on his sleeve, third person may work better.

In *Unexpected Pleasures*, I alternated first-person viewpoint with third-person. April Ruth Bates, who says the first thing that comes to mind, relates her chapters in the first person; in the chapters which feature 32-year-old Foster Williams, the bridge worker, a shy, reserved man of few words, using third person helped me achieve that distance.

The following are two selections from this novel: one at the end of chapter four told from Foster's point of view in third person, the other at the beginning of chapter five told in first person by April Ruth:

(End of chapter four):

" . . . Why Foster, Thomasine, and Dorothy could set themselves up in neon lights, and that still wouldn't be reason enough for anyone to take Earl Bates' youngest away from him. You got yourself stuck with a girl don't have no idea what marriage is about, and Earl is mad as a hornet that he let her go."

Foster heard the words but they did not seem to register. He stared at his uncle blankly, and Russell went on:

"He says Mrs. Dawson got him to sign that paper when he was drinking, and nothing in this world would have made him sign away that girl. He says the first hint you give of mistreating her, he's going after you with a lawyer."

With that, Russell turned and strode back to the house where Shum stood listening, and both uncles marched inside and shut the door.

Foster moved behind the shed and lowered himself down on the lumber. The syllables aligned themselves into words and the words into sentences. He had known long before his uncle opened his mouth, even before the drive to Denton. While the thought was still nebulous in his head, however, he had blown it away like smoke: Mrs. Dawson had not used Foster, Foster had used her. It was easier to pretend that he was saving April Ruth from the juvenile home, it seemed, than it was to admit that he had loved that girl since she was nine—that her isolation there in the trailer had reached out and caught hold of the loneliness in himself. Caught hold and held on.

(Beginning of chapter five)

Only been at Foster's for a week, but it sure felt good heading down that driveway with Dorothy. Passed his uncles on the way, coming from the mailbox. Russell, he keeps walking, pretends he don't even see us at all, but Shum stops, his jaw dropping, head turning right along with the car.

"Hey, mister, put your teeth back in your mouth," Dorothy yells out the window, and when we reach the road, we laugh. "Sure hope Foster doesn't turn out like them when he gets old," she says.

Dorothy don't bleach her hair like Thomasine, lets it hang long and black around her shoulders. She's shorter, too, and you know she's got hips, but her eyes are big and blue and she always smells like cinnamon or something.

"Mrs. Foster Williams," she says, rolling the window up again. Then she gives me the kind of look that means she's going to ask something personal. "So what's he like, April?" I knew she didn't mean how good a talker he was.

"Like most men, I guess," I told her, studying the road ahead.

She watches me a moment, then sighs. "Well, sometimes it's better than others," she says, and shuts up.

Not only does alternating from third person to first in the above selections help bring the personalities of each character to life but the contrast between them is so stark that this gives a hint of the conflict to come. In addition, there is the advantage of being able to describe the same situation from two different perspectives; to show in a later chapter, for example, what April Ruth is doing and thinking after Foster comes home and finds her gone.

A few authors have been successful—some more than others—in having *several* characters within a novel tell the story, each in his own first-person singular voice. The method is less confusing when these changing voices are carefully delineated by scene or chapter, more so when the author switches point of view on the same page or even in the same paragraph. Unless you are very skillful in making these transitions, giving your readers a thorough understanding of one main character works better.

The omniscient voice

At first glance, it may seem that the omniscient point of view would be the best of all possible worlds. You, the author, may jump around from character to character as you please; you may tell what each of your characters is thinking and feeling. Readers may know exactly what Mrs. Donaldson is planning at her end of the table, and in the next paragraph find out what her husband, at the other end, is up to. They may commiserate with one of the Donaldson daughters because she has just been jilted; with the son, whose father doesn't believe he has a brain in his head; and even with the cook in the kitchen who has burned the roast and is afraid to serve it.

Readers are allowed to see everything, hear everything, be in on every secret—to fly to London with the wealthy Donaldson family and come back on the next plane with the nanny.

The omniscient point of view is especially good for novels involving a large cast, as, for example, when you are following two complicated families, showing their history and how they interact. It is useful when a large portrait is being painted of many people first in one city and then another, and you present your characters and their settings on a grand scale.

When the narrative voice—your own—has a special quality, like that of a storyteller's, the omniscient point of view can be very effective: *Now Barbara knew she shouldn't go, of course. . .* is one example. Or even, *Let us suppose that although Barbara knew she shouldn't go . . .* In these cases, the narrator's voice intrudes deliberately and is part of the author's style.

The disadvantage of the omniscient point of view is that, in most cases, it is the least personal or intimate. It isn't as easy for readers to identify strongly with the protagonist if they are also expected to share the inner feelings of other characters. Sometimes it is difficult for the reader to determine just who the main character is. It may seem to be one character in one chapter, another later on. And perhaps this is the way the author wants it. Skilled writers can use the omniscient point of view effectively, but—just as with the other viewpoints—they must have specific reasons for choosing it.

When the idea of a character and plot first comes to us, the voice of the protagonist sometimes comes along with it, and that tells us how we should write the story—possibly in first person. Or we hear instead a narrator's voice—not the main character's—talking about the protagonist, and that seems to be the way to go.

If there is any doubt as to which viewpoint you should use for your novel, try visualizing as many of the scenes to come as you can. Imagine how each of them would read in first person, in third person, from the omniscient point of view. Very often this will help you in selecting the right viewpoint. You may discover that there are so many scenes that would not work well in first person that you choose another vantage point. But if you are still having difficulty, take a paragraph or a page—a chapter, if necessary—and write it from several points of view.

There is a variety of ways to mix and match: You may use the stream-of-consciousness viewpoint, putting words down on paper much in the same way that thought fragments enter the mind; you may portray the flashbacks in first person and the rest of the novel in third person. The guiding rule is clarity. You do not want to sacrifice your story line for an experiment in viewpoints. For beginning novelists especially, it is best to use one of the three basic viewpoints described. Once you master these, you can try new combinations of your own.

❧ 8

Dialogue

IF THE JOY OF FICTION WRITING, for you, is dialogue, you may find yourself rushing through the narrative sections of your novel to get to what you love most—a conversation between characters.

On the other hand, you may prove excellent at writing long paragraphs describing a street or a sunset, but find that words stiffen on paper whenever your characters open their mouths.

Or you may be one of those lucky writers who are good at both dialogue and narrative. Writers' strengths in these areas may have something to do with whether their orientation is primarily visual or auditory, but the good news is that you can train yourself to improve both.

How do people really talk?

Anthony Burgess said that a novelist "writes with his ear." What is needed to write authentic dialogue is not just a good ear for conversation, however, but the ability to "hear" the unspoken feelings as well. In this, as in creating the personalities of your characters, you must become each speaker in turn.

Obviously you will have found out much more about your characters after you've finished the first draft of your novel than you knew when you started. You might even discover you don't much like your protagonist. By going through your manuscript and reading aloud everything a particular character says, you may see that you have portrayed someone, through dialogue, as a whining complainer, when that was not your intention.

There is probably no simpler way to make dialogue ring true than to ask yourself constantly, "What would Sara *really* have said?" or "If I were this person, how would I feel if someone did that to me, and what would I *say?*"

It seems so simple. But it is more than just listening to the way people talk and writing down their words. A marvelous conversation overheard on the bus can rarely be used verbatim in a story. You must skillfully modify and condense real-life dialogue; you must be selective, choosing the exact words to express emotion in the appropriate tone at just the right time. If we recorded real talk just as it is spoken, we would have pages and pages of mundane sentences, of conversations that go nowhere, of "uhs" and repetitions. So what is an author to do?

Those hidden censors

To begin with, forget your censors. Writers often have many invisible people looking over their shoulders. Write your story first, *then* worry about what your great Aunt Minnie would think if she read it. You must be true first of all to your craft.

The following scene from *The Year of the Gopher* would not exactly warm the heart of a Sunday-school teacher, but it is the way some young men talk. (Most of the characters here have both given names and nicknames):

> Dave Hahn was the first one to sound drunk. He's got a slighter build, and alcohol gets to him sooner. He began that wheezing laugh he gets when he's drinking, and I thought,

here we go again: rabbits. But Dave didn't want to talk rabbits this time; he wanted to talk about girls. While the boats bobbed up and down there by the wharf, Dave told us what he and his date had done on prom night in the stateroom of Wally Baisinger's cabin cruiser.

I'd already heard it, but not in such detail. Psycho hadn't heard it at all, and sat motionless, his lips slightly parted.

"Jeez, Dave, rack it up," I said, embarrassed. "I don't want to know every little move." I lied, of course.

Dave took off his jacket and spread it on the grass, then lay down. "But it was this gorgeous little mole—strawberry red—right on the edge of her tit," he said.

Psycho gave a little moan and reached for the vodka again. He slugged some more down.

"You know what?" said Bud, and his voice was a little too loud. "Know what? I heard that girls have a saying . . ." Bud sprawled out on his stomach. "Girls," he said again, his words slightly slurred, "have this saying, that if they don't get laid by prom night, they'll have seven years bad luck."

"Bullshit," I said. "That's a lot of bullshit, Discount. You made that up."

Bud raised up on one hand. "Honest! That's what my date told me. That's exactly what she said."

Dave was laughing again. "So did you put it to her, Discount? You save her from seven years bad luck?"

"Why not?" Discount said, and I knew he was lying. He'd told me the day after the prom that they hadn't gone that far. We were really full of it—all of us.

Only Psycho was silent. Every time the bottle went around, he took three slugs instead of two. I'm not the outsider, I remember thinking. Psycho's the outsider. Marsh hasn't even been out with a girl. Girls haven't been born, as far as he's concerned.

It made me feel better. We were still a team—Dave, Discount, and I. It was Psycho who didn't fit in.

"Hey, Marsh," I said, peering at him from around the tree trunk where we were sitting. "When you going to lay a girl?"

"Oh, shut up," said Psycho, glaring at me.

But the other guys picked it right up.

"Psycho's going to marry his cousin," Bud said, and we all whooped.

"How about *you*?" Marsh said to me. "How about you, Big Mouth? What'd *you* do on prom night? *You* score?"

I'd never talked too much with Marsh about my dates, never wanted him to feel bad—to feel left out. I'd certainly never told him how far I'd gone with Maureen. But this time it was different.

I grinned crazily at the others. "Let's just say that the next morning I had mosquito bites on my butt," I said, and Dave and Discount stared at me wide-eyed, then cheered.

"Way to *go*, Gopher!" Dave said. "How 'bout that?"

Marsh handed the bottle over to Discount and tried to stand up, but it took him two tries. We laughed. He sort of toddled down toward the water.

"Hey, Psycho, going to take a bath?" Dave yelled.

"He's got the hots from all this talk. Going to cool off," I said.

"Fuck off," Marsh said in answer. He grabbed hold of a post on the dock and stood there for some time, his back to us, his head bobbing slightly against the night sky as the water ebbed and flowed. We grinned at each and finished off the bottle.

Forget your English teachers, too. Sometimes people grunt instead of using words. Sometimes they simply make a gesture with their hands. Conversation, real conversation, is interspersed with sounds, gestures, hesitancies, half-sentences, expletives, and often, bad grammar.

The following excerpt from *Unexpected Pleasures* would be a traditional English teacher's nightmare, but if it had been written grammatically correct, the characters would have died on the spot:

. . . April was leaning against the wall, tracing a crack in the plaster with one finger, her ankles crossed.

"Now look here, April. You and me made an agreement we

were going to Denton. You just tell Dorothy you can visit her some other day."

"I'm not going to Denton, Foster, and you can't make me."

"Well, then, maybe you should just get yourself back home to your daddy."

She looked at him, surprised, and studied him for a moment. Then, disentangling her feet, she started down the hall. "All right," she said.

Foster grabbed her arm, but she broke free. He followed her into the bedroom.

"This what you want? You want to leave me?"

"No."

"Well, why you acting this way?"

"Foster, I wasn't never married before. I got to have time to get used to it." She plopped down on the bed.

Anger and exasperation took over once again. "Thomasine put you up to this? Tell you to back off this way?"

"Thomasine thinks we're married. Didn't tell her nothing."

"Jesus Christ." Foster leaned against the door, arms folded over his chest. He stared at her hard. "You do this a lot? Make up your mind to do one thing and go off and do another?"

"You don't want me to stay, Foster, just say so."

"Goddamit, I'm asking you a question, April! You do this a lot?"

"I never lived with a man before, I told you! How do I know what I'm going to do?" she shot back.

Foster let out his breath, turned away, then looked at her again in disbelief.

"I swear to God I don't know what to do with you."

"Want me to go?"

"*No*, damn it! Of *course* I don't."

"Then I'll stay," she said, and went back out to the kitchen.

If your dialogue seems natural and easy in one place but not in another, think, *What would he really say next?* It might be an expletive—the most vulgar kind of expletive, in fact. Or an expletive may be too easy. The emotion may be so great that the character is, for a time at least, speechless.

Differentiating your characters through dialogue

One of the mistakes writers most easily make is to have all of their characters sound alike. Even experienced novelists sometimes make this error. A writer may adopt a certain narrative voice for the novel that carries over into the characters' conversations as well. If the narrative is somewhat pedantic, the characters speak that way also. Or if the author's narrative is clipped, precise, and written for the most part in short phrases, the characters may also tend to talk like that.

Just as you can tell who is talking in a roomful of family members even when your eyes are closed, so should readers, after they get to know your characters, be able to identify the speaker from the dialogue, even without an occasional "he said" or "she replied."

"But they are all well-educated!" a writer might protest when the manuscript is criticized. "They just naturally talk like this." Or, "But they're all Southern women, and this is how Southern women sound."

While it may be true that there are characteristics of speech common to certain groups, there are also individual variations that the writer must highlight if the characters are going to come to life on the page. At a dinner party in your novel, for example, you cannot simply apportion sections of your own philosophy of life to various guests, or they will all seem cut from the same cloth, all equally verbal, all equally profound.

Edward Albee, the playwright, has said that he never begins the writing of a play until he is convinced that each of his characters has developed, in Albee's mind, a vital identity and a voice of his own. One of Albee's methods of testing them is to go for long walks on the beach, taking along with him some of the characters he plans to use. He then invents a new situation not yet in the play. If he can improvise spur-of-the-moment dialogue for the characters in this new situation, then he feels he knows them well enough to go ahead and put them down on paper.

The next time you are in a roomful of people whom you are meeting for the first time, listen carefully. They may at first all sound alike—the men benign, polite, jocular, controlled—the women more talkative, more candid, quicker to argue, quicker to laugh. As the evening progresses, however, you should be aware of decided differences among the guests which were there all the time but took you a while to sort out. Whenever A makes a comment, B— however politely—takes exception. C does not talk much at all, but when he does, he usually has something significant or funny to say. D seems to agree with everyone, E with no one, and F constantly interrupts.

Some people talk fast and fidget as they speak, one foot continually bobbing about, or hands gesturing in front of them. Others speak without moving anything but their mouths, as though bound in a straitjacket. Some talk hesitantly—a few words at a time, then a pause. Others make their observations in rapid-fire delivery. While you don't want to make your characters so different from one another that the effect is disconcerting, what they say or how they say it or what they do with their bodies as they talk must be distinctive enough to give the reader a sense of each of them immediately.

Staying in touch with your characters

Too often it is not that the writer has a tin ear when he writes dialogue, but that he has lost touch with his characters. This is often evident when authors include children in their novels. They may use expressions for their younger characters that were natural forty years ago but would sound out of date today. Whereas a young person may once have said, "That's a keen car," years later he would have said, "That's a neat car," then "That's a bad car," then "That's an awesome car."

It is not only current expressions that can bog a writer down, however. Writers can, after all, easily avoid the use of slang so their dialogue won't sound dated. But writers can also lose touch with the way various types of people or age groups live now—the way they think, the things they do.

A young writer can be out of touch with the elderly; a male writer may discover that he really doesn't understand women well enough to create a female protagonist, and vice versa. This is not an insurmountable problem, but you should be very comfortable with the characters you are writing about.

You may find it helpful to keep your own clipping file of newspaper and magazine articles on any number of subjects that interest you: various age groups, occupations, children's games, teen-age worries, parenthood, and others. In-depth interviews with young mothers, blue-collar workers, nursing home residents, businessmen, junior high students and veterans allow you a glimpse of what they talk about and how they say it, what they do in their spare time, and what concerns them.

Stay in touch with the kinds of characters you are writing about. Go where they are. Listen and observe. Sometimes it doesn't take much. Sometimes just listening to a conversation on a subway, connecting it to a long interview you read in the paper, observing the girl next door, remembering incidents (the *feelings* involved, more than the events) that happened to you at fourteen, make them all come together in your mind to form a flesh-and-blood character in your novel. A time will come in your research when you have absorbed the material so completely that it comes out in an easy flow; the reader would swear that you—the author—*are* a young girl, or a bridge builder, or a native American, or a CPA in New York City, because the dialogue rings true.

Dialect

Using dialect in dialogue is tricky. It involves much more than just filling your pages with double negatives or such regional idioms as "I might could." As writers listen to their characters talk, they must be aware, artistically, of what they, themselves, can and cannot do with dialect. What they can't often do is to duplicate a sentence *exactly* as it would be spoken in dialect in real life. If every "g" were dropped and every double negative recorded, the reader would soon throw down the book in exasperation. "Ah'm thinkin' of goin' to Macon tomorra to git m'self some preachin' clothes," may be exactly the way the old man you knew in Georgia talked, but you'd better not have many lines like this in your novel.

The author must try to sense how he can give just enough of the flavor of the region and no more. How do you know when enough is enough? You read the sentence or the paragraph aloud, over and over again. Whenever something jars, whenever the tongue trips, whenever the mind says "This is a bit much," tone it down. Dialogue too full of "bless my soul" and "sake's alive" will sound like a satire of *Tobacco Road*. The characters will become stereotypes, and the reader's attention will be diverted to all the quaint figures of speech and away from the plot.

In writing *Unexpected Pleasures*, I found April Ruth's dialect especially troublesome because she narrates her own chapters in the first person. Not only was the reader being bombarded with the dropped "gs' and double negatives in her dialogue, but in her narrative as well. The editor suggested at last that we keep her and others' dialect in conversations, but use it sparingly when she narrates. Here is a sample:

> Anytime you don't know whether to be happy or sad, something comes along and decides it for you. We get back from Baltimore, Gus still not knowing, and next morning, in the middle of a snowstorm, I find out about Foster.
>
> It's like I'm there at the top of the bridge with him, like I feel myself slipping over the edge, nothing to hang on to—just emptiness. There I am in the second-floor corridor of the Adams Hotel with the wall phone in my hand, and it's like I can't catch my breath.
>
> "Thomasine," I say finally, "if you was ever a sister to me, you got to drive me to Baltimore right this minute to see Foster."
>
> Thomasine gives a shriek. "There's five inches of snow on the ground, April, and more comin'!"
>
> "You don't drive me there, I'm goin' to walk," I tell her, and she knows I would, too.
>
> Half hour later Thomasine comes over and I slide in the car, my eyes all puffy from crying. She says if she gets killed on the beltway, it's me she's got to thank for it. And all the way there she tells me how it's pity I'm feeling for Foster, not love.
>
> "You wouldn't never have walked out on him, April, if you loved him," she says. "You just got a soft heart for anything sick and suffering."
>
> I just keep right on bawling and don't pay her no mind. Windshield wipers going so fast to keep the snow off make you dizzy. Thomasine looks over at me now and then and grunts.
>
> "You got to quit goin' around with old men, April, and pay attention to the young ones," she warns. "People are startin' to talk about you."
>
> "I don't care one small least little bit," I tell her. "What do they say?"

"Say you're looking for some kind of father, 'cause Daddy
weren't no father to you at all."

"What's so surprising about that?" I ask her.

"Sweet Jesus!" says Thomasine. "It's sick, that's what." I
could've said what kind of sick it is climbing in bed with a bunch
of truck drivers, but it's Thomasine's car getting me to Baltimore, so I just go back to weeping again. Thinking how last
Monday there I was in Baltimore with Gus when Foster was
falling off that bridge. Then all week long, while I'm lying in
that king-size bed in the hotel room, Foster's lying in the
hospital between life and death, and me not even knowing.

As with most of writing, there are no hard and fast rules
about using dialect. Your ear makes the final decision,
which means you must read the section aloud. Don't count
on your eye to do this for you. You must be creative, you
must try different approaches until finally, when you read
the paragraph once again, there is just enough dialect, not
too much, and it seems right.

Making your dialogue do too much

Another thing that may give you difficulty with dialogue
is trying to have it do too much. Instead of letting the
character say what is on his mind, you hire him to do a little
more than the contract calls for. The contract should read,
"Be yourself," but authors often find it convenient to have a
character provide a little background information on himself so that they won't have to do it in the next paragraph.
The character, in essence, is talking to the reader rather
than to someone else in the scene.

This is the sort of thing you see frequently in some comic
strips, where a husband may say to his wife of twenty
years:

"My sister, Charlotte, is coming to visit."
"Oh no! Not the Charlotte who lives in Pittsburgh!"

"Yes. She and her husband Bob were divorced last year."

"And left little nine-year-old Alexander in a boarding school."

"It was all because of that twenty-year-old tramp, Glenda, that Bob took up with."

"And Charlotte so weak from her gall bladder surgery!"

The characters who spoke these lines are obviously alive because we see them in the next frame, but if people talked like that in a novel, they might as well be dead for all the life they would convey. What is so very wrong here is that each is telling what, presumably, the other already knows.

Still, the author's task is not only to let the characters be themselves, but to make everything they say move the story along. This may sound like a contradiction—how can the characters talk normally if they must, at the same time, move the plot forward?—yet if they don't move the plot forward, they may just talk on and on for ten pages to no purpose in the novel.

This is where selectivity comes in. Whatever information is conveyed to the reader must be handled so skillfully that he would never guess you are pulling strings. One way to accomplish this is to use the conversation to reveal feelings as well as to help readers know the characters better, and hence convey far more through the dialogue than information. For example:

"Did you know Charlotte's coming tomorrow?"

"Not tomorrow! She couldn't come at a worse time."

"Maybe she'll just come down for the afternoon."

"You know she won't. She wouldn't want to make a three-hour trip twice in one day, especially a month after gall-bladder surgery."

"It's not that far to Pittsburgh."

"You *always* say things like that! To you, everything is always easier or closer or simpler than it really is! I know she'll stay a week!"

"Be charitable for once in your life."

"Look. I know your sister's hurting—that divorce wasn't easy. And I know she misses Alexander. But a nine-year-old kid away in a boarding school is hurting too, and yet it's always *her* feelings she talks about, *her* problems."

"Bob's going to marry that woman, you know. It's pretty definite."

"That *tramp*, you mean. Well, a man of fifty-five who leaves his wife and marries a woman twenty years old deserves everything he gets, and I'll bet Glenda leads him a merry chase."

Knowing when to stop

With dialogue, you can cover a great amount of material that you otherwise would have to spell out in narrative form. At the same time, there are many pitfalls that can trap you.

As with everything you write, it is as important to know what to leave out as what to put in—when to end the conversation as well as when to begin one. To return again to *Unexpected Pleasures*, April Ruth is talking with Foster, whose uncles have never forgiven him for not going to Vietnam to avenge his brother's death. In this scene, April and Foster are making dinner, and she has asked him point blank why his uncles don't like him. He tells her how they expected him to go to Vietnam, and April, who is telling the story, replies:

"Two dead nephews is better than one?"

"Think I'm a coward," Foster said, and his voice is low and flat like maybe I'd hear it, maybe I wouldn't.

I'm setting the plates on the table and all of a sudden I look over at Foster's back and it's like I'm looking through the layers—like I can see through his shirt and his skin and on into his chest and see it still hurts, what his uncles think of him, whether he says so or not.

"Foster," I says, "your uncles ever fight in a war?"

"No," he says, and lifts out the meat to make gravy.

"They ever work on a bridge, three-hundred feet in the air?"

"No. . . ."

"Well, then," I said. And we had our supper.

Sometimes dialogue is used not only to let our characters speak, not only to convey information and feeling, but also to bring about a resolution of plot. *A String of Chances* provides an example. In this novel, the family consists of Mr. Hutchins, the preacher; his wife, the practical nurse; grumpy Aunt Ida; the oldest sister, Rose, who has been jilted; the middle sister Wilma, who ran off; and Evie, the youngest. Also living in the home is Sister Ozzie, a senile old woman from the church.

At the end of the book, I wanted a scene in which Evie's cousin, Donna Jean Rawley, who has lost her newborn baby, makes her peace with Evie's religious family, whom she has been avoiding for some time, mostly because she married the man that Rose was in love with. I wanted a conversation that would bring the family around full circle, with both poignancy and humor.

In this scene, Evie has persuaded Donna Jean to take part in preserve-making as a way of helping her work through her grief and depression over her baby's death. The women have greeted Donna Jean warmly with hugs, and Donna Jean half-heartedly joins in:

"Help," came a voice from the back bedroom.

"Cartoons is over," Aunt Ida said. "Now Ozzie will want to go to the bathroom and put on her lipstick and take a walk and everything at once, mark my words."

"Evie, you bring her here," Mother said. "Maybe she'd like to watch."

Sister Ozzie was slipping over the edge of the bed.

"Wait a minute," Evie told her, and brought the wheelchair around. Sister Ozzie looked at her hard.

"What are you doing here?" she demanded.

"I'm Evie. Remember?"

"You the one that ran off?"

"No, that was Wilma. I'm going to let you watch us make jam."

Evie pushed the wheelchair to the kitchen and up close to Donna Jean. The tall white-haired woman stared fixedly at the newcomer.

"Who's this?" she asked. "She the one who ran off?"

"That's Donna Jean, Ozzie," said Aunt Ida. "Now you sit here and watch what we're doing, and we'll give you a taste after a bit."

"My mama made jam," said Ozzie, leaning over and peering into Donna Jean's face. "My mama made jam, but she's dead."

Donna Jean paused, the blue-handled masher in her hand, and looked at Ozzie.

"Ozzie, you hush!" said Rose.

"My mama's been dead fifty years, they tell me, and I haven't got over it yet."

Evie stood motionless there in the doorway. For a moment, as Donna Jean looked in the old woman's eyes, it appeared she was about to cry. Then suddenly she reached over and put one hand on Ozzie's. "I lost my mama and baby too, and I don't think I'm ever going to get over it either," she said.

And in one of those rare moments when Sister Ozzie seemed lucid, her own eyes softened and she said, "Well, then, that makes us sisters, doesn't it, and I don't blame you one bit for running off."

Donna Jean smiled and exchanged glances with Rose at the stove, and then smiles traveled about the kitchen. Sister Ozzie leaned back and began to hum.

Using dialogue effectively also means knowing when not to use it—when to let actions convey the words, symbolism represent the thoughts.

Earlier in *A String of Chances*, while Donna Jean is pregnant, she mothers a stray cat that has been hanging around the back door. After her baby dies, the young mother sits on the back step for weeks, unwashed and uncombed; when the yellow cat comes to her for affection, she shoves it away. But by the end of the book, after Donna Jean makes her first tentative effort to mingle with other people again and finds them warm and supportive, she sits once again on the porch step, and this time, when the yellow cat approaches, she leans back and lets it crawl into her lap. Nothing more is needed.

❧ 9

Suspense and Mood: Keeping the Pace

MOOD IS SOMETHING like smoke, wafting into the first paragraph of a novel, then permeating the chapters scene by scene. Except that it doesn't get there by accident; authors put mood into their novels as deliberately as they flesh out a character or outline a plot.

It is true, however, that many authors, when they begin a novel, do not separate in their minds all the various elements of the book they are writing. They do not think one day about style and the next about mood; they don't separate mood from suspense or suspense from emotion. These writers just feel their way along, thinking in terms not so much of plot, style, theme, mood, and suspense, but rather, "How do I want the reader to feel at this point? What do I want him to suspect? How much do I want him to know? What do I need to do to propel him into the next chapter?" And the answers to these questions lie in elements like mood, suspense, style, dialogue, voice, even though the authors are not thinking about these in isolated compartments.

If this sounds mystical, consider the act of ballroom dancing, of riding a bicycle, of making love. There are manuals for all of these things, of course, but when you start listing all the steps in sequence, it sounds a bit foolish. Not that they aren't important. Not that they can be overlooked. But when you are in the act of riding a bicycle or making love, some of what you do comes naturally. You do what feels right. You make accommodations that particularly suit you. And it's the same with writing.

You may start out to tell the story of a great tragedy, and the beginning may contain the seeds of pathos, but when you get to the second chapter, you may discover, to your astonishment, that a little humor is creeping in.

Or perhaps you intended to write a dizzy, farcical account of a European vacation, but discover halfway through that there's a poignancy there you hadn't expected or planned— that it is not only an account of a bachelor's wild adventures, but the tale of a lonely man.

Sometimes we don't know until we get well into a piece of fiction what is needed exactly, or what different moods will evolve. Mood depends partly on plot—whether the book is to be a mystery or a comedy, for example; it depends also on the characters who will be in the story and how the story is told. It depends on the pace, on the degree of suspense that you wish to sustain. It is achieved in part by your choice of words and phrasing. The way the words sound together should make the reader shiver or smile.

Foreshadowing

Suspense, even in a novel of ordinary people—not necessarily a detective story—is a hook, pulling the reader from page to page and chapter to chapter. You must tell only enough to entice, but not nearly enough to satisfy, not until The End, anyway. You should never tell your readers any more than they must really know at that particular moment.

You allude to minor matters not yet fully understood by the reader. You drop subtle hints. "She did not know, till she got in the car, what lay ahead," will keep us interested even though the next four pages may describe what and how she packed that morning, if, of course, this proves necessary. And then, a single word here and there will provide clues that something unexpected is coming: "fierce shadows on the grass . . ."; "trees stood like soldiers . . ."; "the gloom of dusk . . ." Adjectives or phrases break into a pastoral setting like the discordant notes in a Kurt Weill composition: It *seems* as though the mood is peaceful or happy, but somehow readers get the feeling that all is not well.

In *The Year of the Gopher,* cited earlier, George Richards and his friends are drinking by the lake, and the prevailing mood at first is humorous. The young men are bragging about their sexual exploits, real and imagined. Every so often, though, a serious note intrudes: George has usually been protective of his friend Marsh (Psycho), but in this scene, he begins taunting him. Marsh gets up and totters down to the water. While the conversation still remains humorous, the reader has intimations of danger. As the drama continues, the boys' own awareness that they ought to leave becomes the drumbeat:

> Marsh let go of the post finally and walked along the wharf. Then he jumped down onto the deck of the first boat, tied a few feet away.
>
> "Psycho, get your ass out of there. They're likely to come back any minute," I yelled.
>
> Marsh made no reply. We sat up and watched him. He was peering through the glass doors into the cabin. We laughed some more, and Psycho clowned around.
>
> He climbed up on the bridge next and, leaning to one side, his hand against the cabin, made his way around the boat.

When he had come full circle, he stood up on the edge of the deck, and with a loud "hi-yahhh!" leaped across three feet of water and onto the deck of the second boat.

We were cracking up, and Marsh seemed to enjoy the attention. He could be crazy too, he seemed to be saying. He, too, could be a little wild. From where we sat, we could see him exploring the second boat, going up the ladder to the captain's chair at the very top, sitting awhile, then coming back down to peek in the cabin windows.

"Wouldn't it be a riot if there was some woman in there naked and she saw Marsh looking at her?" Bud said, and we were off again, almost sick with laughter. When you're drunk, you laugh at anything. The boat bobbed gently up and down, and we thought of all that vodka in Psycho's stomach. We laughed some more.

"He is going to be one sick dude," Bud observed. "I hope he doesn't heave on their deck chairs."

I was keeping one eye on the path leading up to the Beach Club. "Maybe we'd better go," I said.

"Who's going to drive?" Bud asked.

"We could just walk around awhile," I suggested. We got up and shook the grass off our coats. "Psycho!" I yelled. "Come on, now—we're going to walk around the lake."

Marsh only gave a whoop and went sailing through the air toward the third boat. One foot didn't quite make it, and we heard it scrabbling against the side of the boat as he tumbled onto the deck.

"C'mon, Marsh," I called again. "We're going to walk off the vodka."

Psycho only climbed up on the deck bench and with another "hi-yahhh!" leaped across the deck to the opposite bench. He teetered for a moment, then jumped down and began checking out the windows of the third cabin.

"Someone's coming, Psycho," Dave fibbed.

"We're going, Marsh," I called. We slung our jackets over our shoulders and walked a little way up the path.

"Hi-yahhh!" came Psycho's voice again. We saw him poised

against the sky as he made the leap over to the second boat again, but this time it was followed by silence, then a splash.

"Jesus!" said Discount.

"Psycho?" I yelled.

Dave gave a short laugh. We waited.

"Marsh!" I yelled again, and started down to the water.

Suddenly Bud was running past me, kicking off his shoes, unbuckling his belt. I saw his pants drop, saw his body hit the water. None of us should have been in the lake.

I grabbed hold of the post and lowered myself down onto the first boat, then crawled over into the second, blinking my eyes, trying to clear my head. There was furious splashing, and Bud emerged between the second and third boats, his eyes huge and frightened.

"Is he down there?" I asked.

Bud didn't answer, just ducked under again.

"Is he there?" Dave yelled from the wharf. "Should I go for help?"

I peered over into the water. It was dark as chocolate pudding. I could hear it, but I couldn't see it. Bud came up again, and his mouth sagged as though he were crying. He dived down a third time.

"*Call* somebody!" I yelled to Dave. Then I stripped off my pants and went over the side.

Sometimes the combination of two moods—the dominant mood we want for the scene and its opposite—serves to emphasize the major mood all the more. Think of the impact of a movie chase scene through an amusement park, especially if the villain happens to be the murderer of young children. Here one might combine the horror of a child-murderer with the delight of young children on an outing. The horror would be intensified by juxtaposing quick takes of the murderer stalking a child against scenes of children laughing with pleasure; flashes of children's excited faces against flashes of the murderer's boots slogging through the mud; children's screams as the roller coaster thunders down a precipitous slope, then the murderer's hand clasping a knife.

A writer can use the same technique in a novel, inserting small, casual details in a scene of tension: For instance, a woman holds a gun in her lap while her companion, across the table, studiously butters his bread. Readers know that probably nothing will happen as long as a servant is standing by, but their sense of foreboding mounts.

You may also use delaying tactics to establish interest in a character. He might be talked about pages or even chapters before he makes his entrance, so that readers can scarcely wait until he can be seen. They are told so many bad things about him that they hate him before he appears. Or better yet, the writer or other characters in the story may say very contradictory things about him, so readers are not sure what to expect or believe.

In foreshadowing events to come, you may have your characters express their fervent desires, thus instantly creating in readers the fear that something will happen to prevent these wishes from coming true.

In *A String of Chances*, for example, before Donna Jean Rawley, the agnostic, loses her baby, there is a scene in which she is happily working to turn a downstairs room of her house into a shop for hand-crafted items. She plans to run the shop with the help of her cousin Evie:

> Joshua seemed to know that he was being talked about because he babbled at them from his infant seat across the floor, blowing little bubbles of spit, his eyes focused on a beam of sunshine coming through the window.
>
> Donna Jean crawled over the newspapers to her baby. Leaning over him, her face seemed a polka-dot fabric all its own, the faint tan freckles contrasting sharply with the clear pink of Joshua's skin.

"Hi, old buddy," she said softly, holding out a finger for him to grasp. "What do you think—are the cousins going to make it or not?"

Joshua tilted his face upwards, captivated by hers, his mouth working vigorously, eyes smiling, cooing out a welcome.

She swept him up in her arms and held him high above her, little feet dangling, then brought him down and hugged him hard. "Oh, Evie, if I ever believed there was a God, it's when I hold this baby. I never had a more wonderful gift in my life."

Here the drum beat begins, the mere wisp of a warning. A worry, perhaps. What would she do if something ever happened to that child? the readers may wonder.

While you may want to use adjectives to foreshadow events, describing sounds in the distance, physical sensations of cold or dampness, you can also achieve a sense of horror by accenting the ordinary, offhand remarks that seem to have no relevance at the moment, but which come back to haunt readers later. When I came to the place in my novel where Joshua Rawley was to be found dead, I used time of day and mundane events to heighten the tension:

It was Thursday the tenth when it happened. For days afterwards, Evie had stared at the calendar, at that single square of white, with nothing more innocuous than "call store about paint" scribbled in pencil.

Twelve fifteen: Chris stopped by with a quart of milk and a submarine sandwich. Evie sat on the swing while he ate, holding Josh on her lap, his bare feet in her hands. . . . (A one-page scene follows.)

One ten: Donna Jean had just given Josh his bath. While he was being diapered, Evie picked up the rubber kitten she had bought him, holding it above his face and squeezing it to make a loud squeak . . . (Another scene).

Four fifty-two: Tom was home . . . (And again there is another domestic scene, an ordinary day in an ordinary family. . . .)

Five twenty-one: "We need a break," Donna Jean said. "I'm going to wake Josh up, or he'll be all off schedule. Evie, do we have any lemonade left from lunch? Let's go out on the porch awhile."

If only time had stopped there. The details of what happened next were imprisoned forever in Evie's head: the feel of the cold pitcher in her hands as she lifted it from the refrigerator, the calendar there above the sink, the sound of Donna Jean's footsteps on the stairs, and Tom opening his briefcase on the dining room table . . .

"Tom!"

Donna Jean's voice sounded choked, raspy, dry, as though words were caught in her throat. Evie set the pitcher on the table and came out of the kitchen to find her cousin halfway down the stairs, leaning against the wall, doubled over, hands on her abdomen, as though she had been kicked. Her face was as white as cream.

"Donna Jean?" Tom came in from the next room.

And suddenly Donna Jean threw back her head, her throat thick, the muscles straining, and her lips opened wide without a sound, as though even a scream could not get through.

Tom grabbed her: "Donna Jean!"

The scream came: "Josh!"

As the clock ticks on readers know that something awful is about to happen. Because of what went on just before these scenes—a quarrel between Evie and her friend Matt—one half suspects that Matt has been killed in an accident. But as the clock continues ticking, and each scene has some mention of Josh, anxiety mounts, readers suspect, they hope it won't happen, and then that awful scream, "Josh!" and they know that it did.

Foreshadowing can be nothing more than letting the reader know that the protector will be out of town or out of the house or even out of the room for a brief time. In a novel about a young married couple living in an apartment complex, for example, let's say there is a rapist at large in the neighborhood. Ted is fearful for Marsha, of course, but then he is sent on a business trip for a week, and the drumbeat begins. The reader's pulse quickens and so does the pace of the story.

Foreshadowing a frightening climax is important. If out of the blue somebody leaps out from behind a door, your reader is frightened for only two seconds. But if Marsha enters the apartment building and calmly goes up the same stairs she has gone up every day, and the reader realizes that the rapist might possibly be up there waiting for her, the suspense becomes almost unbearable, the mood terrifying, even though the sun may be shining and birds singing.

Suspense will be heightened even more if, when someone *does* leap out at Marsha, it is not whom the reader expects. Make it a child playing a game; a cat, perhaps. Readers will breathe a sigh of relief, but they will also get a taste of things to come, making the suspense all the greater; now forewarned, they will watch every nook and cranny. But the rapist is *not* waiting under the steps. Readers will be in total shock when a delivery man passes Marsha on the stairs and his hand reaches out to grab her.

Anticipation plays a large part in both happiness and terror. One great thing about Christmas, for example, is the preparation that goes on so long in advance. The frightening thing about a brain operation is thinking of what might go wrong. And when readers suspect that something dreadful is in store for them, they zip through the pages, wanting to rush out to meet it, eager to get it over with.

Variety

Keeping up the pace in a plot, however, is more than withholding information or stringing the reader along or dropping hints of things to come. Too much of a good thing can grow tiresome. A knife-wielding murderer stalking a child through an amusement park is terrifying for a time, but if it goes on too long, the audience—or the readers—are likely to go out for popcorn. Like a variety show in which a blues singer is followed by a comedian who is in turn followed by a dancer, the scenes in a novel must also keep changing to sustain the interest.

Following the death of a central character, readers do not need scene after scene of mourning; they need some relief. This might come in the form of a character who is not mourning at all, but instead is doing something inappropriate in the situation, something seemingly irreverent: checking his datebook, unwrapping a piece of gum.

If your novel deals with a three-generation family, you might intersperse your chapters about what the young people are doing with a tender love scene between the elderly couple; a little later we need to know what the middle-aged cousins are up to.

If you want to create unrelieved suspense or even fear, how do you give readers—and yourself, as well—a respite without breaking the taut mood entirely? Again, you do it with that soft, distant drumbeat that says, *Don't be fooled;* you can use the adjective that jars: "a tepid smile," a loving touch that makes the reader wonder.

The mother of a disturbed young girl, for example, arrives home from work each day fearful that her daughter may have committed suicide. On this particular day, however, the daughter greets her warmly and gives her a rose. Readers sigh with relief. And yet. . . ? Is this a good sign? A bad sign? The writer may give a brief but wary respite by having the daughter make a remark that could be taken either way: "Starting tomorrow, Mother, your life is going to be a lot happier." We feel strangely chilled, yet nothing has happened; the daughter is still smiling.

You want to lull the reader into a false sense of security. Marsha, for example, who was grabbed by the rapist but escapes, lies awake all night worrying that he might return. Nothing happens that night or the next or the next, and then, just when she decides she can cope with her husband being gone. . . !

Changing scenes, cutting dialogue, shifting to another mood or another tone are all techniques writers use for adding variety to their novels and keeping the pace. It is something at which you can improve with experience.

Reading back over what you have written, preferably aloud, you must ask yourself, "How much of this is really important? How much of this could wait? As the reader, when would *I* want something new to happen, a shift of scene?"

Variety in sentence structure and length helps hold the reader's interest. Three paragraphs on a single page beginning with "She went" are two paragraphs too many. Too many "he saids" and "there weres" produce monotonous writing. In dialogue, shift words around to avoid repeating the same pattern. Consider the following:

> She put one hand on his arm. "I believe you," she said.
> He looked at her in amazement. "But the newspaper. . . ?" he began.
> She leaned back in her chair. "You're the only one who knows the whole story, and it's you I choose to believe," she told him.

And consider how it could be improved:

> She put one hand on his arm. "I believe you," she said.
> "But the newspaper. . . ." He looked at her in amazement.
> "You're the only one who knows the full story," she told him, leaning back in her chair, "and it's you I choose to believe."

Balance is important—balance between narrative and dialogue, between drama and comedy, between action and reflection, men and women, a slow leisurely pace and scenes of page-turning excitement. But don't make it obvious to the reader. The novel must flow naturally and not seem a mechanical see-sawing between slow and fast or funny and serious.

How problems help

Problems are essential to keeping the pace. Not just one problem, either. The central character usually faces a major conflict, but even as he goes about solving it, others crop up.

Writers sustain suspense by throwing in red herrings, not only in mysteries but in almost any novel. Will the protagonist take this road or that one? There are signs pointing both ways. What will the main character do to resolve a conflict, A or B? There are reasons for doing either.

If readers see from the outset what the problem obviously is, and there is only *one* good solution with no real obstacles in the way, why should they read further? If, however, readers must guess not only which road the main character will choose, but, once chosen, how he will travel it, they will have more than one reason to read to the end of the novel.

Which, in fact, is the better road, or should either be taken at all? A man learns that his sister needs a kidney transplant, and that he is the only possible donor. Should he agree to the operation, knowing it could cost him his life— certainly one of his kidneys? If this is all there is to the plot, readers will nod and say yes, the noble thing, of course, would be for him to make the sacrifice.

But what if he has always hated this sister? Should he still do it? Can he live with himself if he doesn't? The readers are probably still nodding: Yes, the noble thing would be to go ahead and be a donor.

Suppose, however, that not only *he* hates her, but the entire community does as well. She has never, in anyone's recollection, done a good deed for another person in her life. In fact, her gossip and maliciousness have broken up more marriages and ruined more families than they can count. If she were dead, the community might feel relieved. What then? Would this sacrifice on the part of her brother possibly change her and therefore be worth the price?

So to make it more difficult, let's say that this man has just lost his wife and has three small children to support. Should he *still* risk it? Don't make it too easy for either the leading character or the readers.

From the climax on

To maintain the suspense, the mood, and the pace in your novel, you should make the reader aware of how one event leads to another; he may not understand right away how the scenes are connected, but he should be able to determine from your writing that, with patience, he will find out.

Flannery O'Connor said she had an aunt "who thinks nothing happens in a story unless somebody gets married or shot at the end of it." Yet the climactic scene may be as dramatic as a house bursting into flame, with all the occupants in it, or as low-key as a character standing at an open door, then turning around and deciding not to walk through it. But whatever you have chosen as the high point of the book, the turning point—the point at which your main character "comes to realize," to change, to make a decision—must pack a wallop. If the reader does not hold his breath, he should at least get a lump in the throat or a feeling of relief or regret or resignation.

Think of the writing process, from the beginning of your novel to the climax, as akin to climbing a mountain—with pauses and backtracking (flashbacks) now and then, but still moving upward. Once the climax or summit is reached, imagine your character skiing down the other side. Events now must move swiftly. Don't dawdle, like a guest at the door having trouble saying goodbye. Don't do much, if any, summing up of what the plot or theme was about. It should have been written so well that your readers know without your telling them. If you would prefer to have them think about it awhile, write it so subtly that they will dwell on it for some time after they have finished the book.

But the finale should not be like a Beethoven symphony that you keep thinking is ending, only to hear another blast from the wind instruments. Some writers, of course, add a plus: a little fillip, something unexpected right at the end, a sort of post-climax. No reader is going to fault you for that.

The end is the end, however, and if you absolutely *must*, you could always write an epilogue or a sequel. But your ending should be satisfactory even if it is tragic, even if it is purposely ambiguous. It will not be satisfactory if you were lazy and made the whole uproar a simple case of mistaken identity. It will not please your reader to discover that the source of the terrifying sounds and events was a deranged man playing a tape in the attic. Don't keep an editor reading for three hundred pages only to have him discover that the main character had an overactive imagination, but you, the author, had none.

✣ 10

Emotion: The Humorous and the Tragic

THE ONE THING THAT WILL make the difference between a mediocre novel that is read and immediately forgotten and a book that is read and remembered is the emotion it evokes in the reader. And that is determined by what the characters in the novel are feeling and how this is portrayed.

If there is not enough emotion, the characters will not seem to care very much about what happens to them, and the reader will not care at all. If there is too much, the story will seem maudlin or sentimental and will lose the reader through overkill.

Making the reader care

Putting in just the right amount of emotion in the right way is an art, not a science, and how this is done is difficult to describe.

When my novel *A String of Chances* was accepted for publication and the job of revision began, my editor wrote a long letter of suggestions to me, including the following:

. . . Somehow it begins a bit too slowly, and it is not as memorable as it ought to be. The pieces of the book don't sort

together and come out as being part of a whole that means
more than the sum of the parts. Basically I think this is
because the emotions, in particular Evie's emotions and won-
derings and problems, do not come through quite as strongly
as they ought to to bind the whole together. It is emotion that
makes a book memorable. It is emotion that makes a book
come alive. And somehow in spite of the very, very deep
problems that occur in this book, the emotions of the reader
are not stirred. Even the death of the baby is somehow removed enough from the reader that the reader is not touched.
Somehow you need to make the emotional life of that book
come across to the reader more effectively. If you can do this, it
will be a very powerful book indeed. It is basically Evie's
emotions that might reach across that barrier between the
character and the reader, but it is everybody's feelings, including Rose's, that must breathe life into your characters.

How this is done is not easy to communicate. Different
writers do it in different ways. But mostly the secret lies, I
think, in choice of words and even more in patterns of words
and cadences of expression. It is a subliminal sort of approach
that catches at the reader without his knowing it. It also lies in
making a reader totally a part of the scene.

I suspect that in this book you want to have some distance
between your reader and your book because it is a thoughtful
book, a probing book, a book that is really exploring the transition of a girl's thinking, rather than her emotions from childhood to adolescence. Yet at the same time, if it is a book that is
going to catch readers and hold them and make them think too,
it must also capture their emotions. Even if they don't feel
directly with the characters, they must understand what the
characters are feeling and see the emotions as effectively as the
mental growth . . . .

It can be very helpful to stop periodically as you write
your novel and ask yourself questions to make sure that you
have not gone off the track:

• What is the main feeling I want to leave with the reader
at the end of the novel? Anger at a social injustice? Grief,

but acceptance, of an opportunity lost? Admiration for a courageous community?

• How well have I prepared the reader for this? Have I subtly planted the seeds of this emotion up to this point without actually calling it by name or being heavy-handed? Have I assumed that it's there when it's really quite murky?

• Do I show my main character experiencing this emotion? Have I focused throughout on what he or she is thinking?

• How do I want the reader to react to my protagonist? With tolerance? Sadness? Ambivalence? Affection? Have I done enough with this character to induce that feeling in the reader without overdoing it?

Making use of the opposite emotion

It is often the juxtaposition of sadness and happiness that makes a tragedy more wrenching—the crying clown; the children playing on a hill in a cemetery while a burial is taking place below; the frozen congratulatory smile of a man who shakes the hand of a rival. A laughing clown is not nearly as humorous as a serious one; a crying child touches us, but not as deeply as the child who is trying valiantly not to cry.

Chekhov, writing on detachment and involvement, put it this way: "When you depict sad or unlucky people and want to touch people's hearts, try to be colder—it gives their grief a background against which it stands out in sharper relief." And he goes on to say that the writer does, and must, suffer with his characters, but he "must do this so the reader does not notice it. The more objective, the stronger will be the effect."

It is almost as difficult to predict what will make people cry as what will make them laugh. And most of us know what variation there is in what is considered humorous. During a tragic scene in a play, you may possibly hear a sob in the audience, but more likely you will just see people dabbing their eyes with a tissue. Perhaps you will see and hear nothing at all. Their grief is being experienced internally, silently.

During a comedy, laughter is loud and evident. Actors frequently say that during a preview performance, when an audience views the play for the first time, the most surprising thing to the actors is where the laughter comes. There may be lines in the play that they were sure would produce spontaneous laughter, yet the audience remains silent; at other times—where the actors predicted the audience would merely smile—a roar of laughter greets them from across the footlights. Discovering at what points laughter is likely to come is one reason for preview performances. And yet, as every actor will also tell you, audiences differ from night to night, and because one audience laughed at the opening line of the second act does not mean that another audience will.

There is a thin line between laughter and tears. "She laughed until she cried" is a common expression. In *Revelations*—the story of a 34-year-old single woman who takes an orphaned young nephew under her wing—Mary and Jake, the nephew, have been invited to an all-too-stuffy restaurant for Thanksgiving dinner with an all-too-stuffy admirer of Mary's named Milt. Jake does not like the man, finds him humorless and pompous; Mary herself is not all that taken with him, but, to be kind, accepts the invitation. The conversation has not gone well to this point, and finally something starts Jake giggling, then laughing, then howling hysterically:

> Mary watched her nephew in both embarrassment and concern. The laughter had become self-perpetuating. The sound of one outburst seemed to spark another. She handed him her

napkin and he covered his mouth, but by now half the diners
had turned to stare. Milt feigned total unconcern and went on
eating, his face beet red, and at the sight of this tremendous
display of fake calm, Jake suddenly howled again, his stomach
pulled violently in, his shoulders shaking. His face was contorted. He was in agony.

Mary reached over and put one hand on his arm, and for a
moment it seemed to have a calming effect. The laughter
stopped, and Jake wiped his eyes. At that very moment, however, the head waiter appeared with a coughdrop on a large
white plate and asked Jake if he thought that would help.

Instantly, a wild shriek filled the dining room, and Jake
doubled over again. He was beyond control.

"Let's go outside, Jake," Mary said sympathetically, and
stood up. "We'll take a walk somewhere."

The young boy staggered awkwardly to his feet, convulsed,
tears streaming down both cheeks, and they made their way
through the tables of gawking patrons till at last they were
outside.

Almost as soon as the door closed behind them, Jake's laughing stopped. He leaned weakly against the building, hands on
his sides, miserable.

"I don't know what got into me, Aunt Mary," he apologized,
humiliated. "That's never happened before in my whole life! Oh,
Christ! I'm so embarrassed. I'll bet Milt's furious!"

Though the reader may smile a little at the memories this
scene evokes, the emotion most likely engendered here is
pain. Readers are uncomfortable with all this hilarity. Yet,
being in Jake's shoes, they can understand it.

Restraint

Restraint is a necessary element in evoking emotion—
the fact that a character is trying so hard *not* to show
feeling makes readers, perverse as they are, feel it all the
more. In *A String of Chances*, when his four-month-old

baby dies, the young father does not spend the night on his knees weeping profusely, but instead wraps the small body in a blanket and takes his dead son around the backyard, introducing him to the big oak, the small garden, the bird feeder, the shed—all the things he had planned to show Josh later.

Restraint in what is said as well as in what is done is equally important.

In my novel *Alice in Rapture, Sort Of,* a twelve-year-old girl who is being raised by her father and older brother calls her Aunt Sally in Chicago whenever she needs advice because she doesn't know whom else to ask. And Aunt Sally tries her best, but usually falls short of being helpful. The following conversation, as related by Alice, takes place when one of her friends tells her that lying down beside a boy, even if nothing happens, is a sin, and Alice asks her aunt about this. Alice is obviously interested in just how far she can go with boys, but if she came right out and asked, it wouldn't be funny:

"I'm so glad you asked me that," Aunt Sally said. She always says that. I could call her at four in the morning to ask about breathing in when you kissed and she'd still say she was glad I'd asked.

"Actually," said Aunt Sally, "a girl could get under the covers with a boy and spend the whole night and it could be an act of mercy, pure and simple."

"It *could?*" I said, getting interested.

"Let's say there was a blizzard," said Aunt Sally, "and there was this boy and girl somehow stranded in this farmhouse, and there was no wood for the fire and only one bed and one blanket. Huddling against each other there in bed would be a simple act of mercy."

"What about if there *wasn't* a blizzard?" I asked.

Incongruity

One of the many ways to evoke laughter is to take a commonplace situation and expand on it: A husband and wife giving a dinner party mull over names of prospective guests. As they veto first one couple and then another because this one's husband is too loud or that one's girlfriend is argumentative, they finally discover there are no satisfactory couples left, and debate the possibility of giving a singles party.

Another way to add humor is to introduce an element of irreverence: a group of nuns quarreling over what to do with the profits from a church bingo game, or a family faced with the prospect of carrying out the wishes of the deceased—to scatter his remains by helicopter over a nudist colony in the San Fernando valley.

The juxtaposition of two radically different people or events or things often produces humor: the prim matron seated next to a man who is picking his teeth; a revival meeting taking place across the street from a brothel; a drugstore display of "Nights of Passion" perfume next to bunion cream and Kaopectate. In each instance the reader finds it amusing because something is out of place, does not belong.

In a scene in *Unexpected Pleasures*, April and Thomasine have gone to the apartment of their prostitute sister who was recently murdered, and are sorting out her things, deciding which they will keep for themselves and which should be given away. April, telling the story, says: "Thomasine sets to work dividing up Dorothy's clothes, but I didn't have the heart for it. Dorothy's feet so small neither one of us could wear her shoes. Fifty-seven pair of four-inch heels with bows and sequins going to the Disabled American Veterans . . . ."

Timing

Timing is still another factor in evoking emotion—knowing when to start and when to quit, where to insert a particular phrase. Should Peter Gaffney say "My god!" before or after he sinks down in the chair? When he opens the door to find his neighbor obviously drunk or after the neighbor goes home? When he finds a certain letter in his mailbox or after he reads it?

You must try on these different hats, shuffle words about, move them from the beginning to the end of sentences, think about whether a certain line would be more effective or dramatic or humorous if it ended quickly on a one-syllable word or were drawn out in a rather pedantic way. You should read the sentences aloud to yourself this way and that, taking out a phrase, adding a phrase. Play it by ear, and it is your ear that will tell you when you've got it right.

To touch your reader, you should take him by surprise. This is not to say that he does not sense that something is going to happen, that he is in for a laugh or is going to be shocked. But if you play your hand too soon, your crucial scene or your punch line loses its impact.

Readers resent being told how to feel; they may also, if told in advance, expect more from a scene than what they get. You should never announce an emotion in advance. You must not say, for example, before a scene takes place, "There in the room was the saddest thing she had ever observed," because that makes for melodrama, and melodrama may make readers snicker.

If you say, "The most hilarious thing happened to Joseph on Saturday," your readers might say to themselves, "*That's* hilarious?" Better to describe what happened and let the reader get an unexpected laugh. We are uncomfortable with comedians who laugh at their own jokes, who say, in effect, "C'mon, laugh!" It is the surprise element that allows readers and audience to feel tragedy or comedy or anger or jealousy in their own way.

Still another insight into humor comes from Richard Armour: "The humor writer must, I think, love the human race, and not in spite of its defects, but because of them. He cannot write anything lastingly, universally, and meaningfully funny out of hatred or out of a feeling of superiority."

Empathy if not sympathy
In the course of a novel, your protagonist may do or say many things of which your readers do not approve. This is all right; they don't have to like what Mary does, but they do have to understand why she did it, no matter how base the lust, how unreasonable the anger, how selfish the envy, how irreverent the humor, or how undeserved the joy. If a character behaved a certain way, then obviously something set her off. And a character can recognize an emotion at the same time she is trying to talk herself out of it, even as she is hating herself for it. She may acknowledge that she has no right to feel this way, yet she *does*, and you must help the reader empathize.

In *Revelations*, Mary has fallen in love with a traveling evangelist, Murray Dawes. Concerned about her, Liz, Mary's sophisticated friend, pays a visit:

"I didn't mean to lecture, Mary. I'm concerned, that's all."
"What's there to be concerned about? Am I concerned about what might happen with you and Greg? Do I come driving down to your apartment to make sure you know what you're doing?"
"Greg and I have been seeing each other for months, Mary. With you, it's all new . . . ."
The contrast, intentional or not, made a sharp cut.

"Little Mary Martha may get herself a man after all, is that it? And who will there be to pity if she does?"

"Mary, that's unfair. When have I ever said anything like that?"

"It's implied, Liz."

"There's nothing I want more for you. You deserve it. You've got it coming! But for God's sake, Murray could be one of those fly-by-night evangelists that absconds with all the money! He could have a wife and seven kids! How long have you known him? Two days? Three?"

"All my life," Mary said. "I feel I've known him all my life."

Liz put one hand over her eyes, then dropped it limply. "Listen, Mary. He may be the greatest guy who ever lived. He may be perfect for you. But give yourself time, huh?"

"You don't see me packing, do you? I've got Jake, remember?"

"Yes. Thank goodness for Jake. At least he'll help keep your feet on the ground."

The cut grew deeper. Liz had evoked his name like an ally. Liz the Sophisticate and Jake the Sensible united against the ridiculous whims of a maiden aunt.

"What is it really, Liz? Jealousy?"

"*Jealousy?* Mary, there's no hidden motive here, believe me. It's just that yesterday—the way you looked, the way you smiled, the way you talked—I've never seen you look like that before, so full of love and joy and expectancy. I just couldn't bear to have you hurt. I'd like to know that Murray feels the same way about you."

Mary heard, but the words were like barbs, sticking against the sides of her head, sharp and unwanted.

"Why is that so unbelievable?" she said, and felt her throat constricting. "He's too marvelous, is that it? Strong, sexy, intelligent, kind . . . .How could he fall for a scared, unsophisticated country girl like Mary?"

"I didn't mean that at all."

"Then what did you mean?" The words came tumbling out. "You couldn't stand that it was my hand he held so long there in

the church yesterday, not yours? My face his eyes kept return-
ing to again and again, not yours? Is that it? It's you who's been
invited away for weekends in Charlottesville, you the doctors
and interns always ask out, you who is so goddamned extro-
verted you can pick out any man you choose and have him
licking your breasts, but it's me that Murray Dawes is interested in this time, and suddenly you can't stand it. Suddenly
you're drenched with concern." She could not believe herself—
could not believe she was sitting there talking that way to Liz.

There are times you need to portray not only one
character's emotions, but those of several different people
in the same scene. You don't need to have everyone say
something in order to do this. Some will talk, others will
just sit, others may say a word or two, but when the scene
is concluded, the reader should know what each character
was feeling.

In the following scene from *The Year of the Gopher,*
George's parents have just discovered that he sabotaged his
applications to the Ivy League schools, all of whom have
rejected him. The mother is hurt, the father is furious, the
brother and sister are in shock, but George has a cause:

"*Why,* George?" Mom was saying. "Why did you do it?"

"Because I didn't want to go," I told her. My teeth felt as
though they were clamped together, as though my jaws had
locked. I actually had trouble talking. Little pains shot up the
side of my cheek.

"You got on that plane with me knowing you were going to
pull something like this?" Dad asked. "You went through that
charade of visiting those schools, secretly sabotaging things at
every turn?"

"George, if you didn't want to go, why didn't you just say
so?" Mom asked.

"I said it every way I knew how, but you weren't listening," I
told her, and now *I* was shouting. My voice didn't sound like
mine at all, though—hollow and high, like someone in a tower.

Ollie stared at me as if I were somebody else. Jeri, sitting back on the stairs, didn't move a muscle. All eyes were on me. "You don't care about me, you don't care about my education, you only care how it makes *you* look!" I said.

"That was totally uncalled for," said Mother, and there were tears in her eyes.

In order not to see the tears, to not even think about them, I went on yelling. "*Somebody* had to make the break. I'm not going to end up at an Ivy League school with a bottle of Maalox just to please you and Dad."

"George, that's unfair!"

But I was unstoppable now. The words came tumbling out: "Take a good look, Mom. Trish is having stomach problems, Ollie's got a tic . . . ."

"George!"

"Somebody had to break the chain. And you want to know something else? I'm not going to college at all next year. Not even the University of Minnesota."

Dad slowly got to his feet, as though he didn't quite trust himself not to rush me. "Okay, you've said it," he said, and his words seemed like chunks of concrete clunking to the floor. "You're my son, and I'm responsible for your food, shelter, and medical care, but beyond that, you're on your own. You want to live your life without any help from me, you've got it. Anything you want beyond the mere necessities, you buy yourself. Is that understood?"

"Yes," I said, my heart still pounding. "Understood."

"Good," Dad said. He turned and strode out of the room, his legs moving rigidly from the hip sockets as though the knees wouldn't bend.

Mom slowly straightened the papers and finally she stood up, too.

"George, how could you?" she said bitterly, and without waiting for an answer, followed Dad out of the room.

My eyes met Ollie's. They were large and scared. I wanted to say something to him about how I hoped this would make things easier for him and Jeri, but it sounded too righteous somehow. I crossed the room and started up the stairs where Jeri was still sitting in exactly the same position she'd been before. She was staring up at me, a dazed expression on her face. She drew her legs up tight to let me pass, and I went in my room and lay on my back till it was time for bed.

When the May issue of the school newspaper came out, it carried the names of all the seniors and what they planned to do after graduation.

Marshall Evans, University of Minnesota . . .David Hahn, Oberlin College . . . Bud Irving, Carnegie-Mellon . . . George Richards, work.

A successful book will not necessarily make a reader laugh aloud or weep. The emotion evoked may be so subtle that the reader may know only, when he puts the novel down at last, that in some way it touched him, moved him, made him recall feelings he had forgotten or things he would like to share.

But it must never make the reader say, "So what?" as though what happened to these characters made no difference. It must make a difference, or the story is not worth telling.

🌀 11

Style and Structure

STYLE IS TO A NOVEL what personality is to the author. A person may be humorous or pedantic or self-effacing or clever, and so may a book. Style is the way authors choose to tell their stories—the manner, the mode, the tone.

The words they select to achieve this play a part, but vocabulary is not all of it. The mood of the story also has something to do with style, but mood tells us more about the story, and style reflects the author. Structure is closely linked with style, but structure is the arrangement of the different parts of a novel, and style depends on more than the way the story is put together.

If, after reading a novel, your comment is that the subject matter was interesting, but the writing is deadly dull, it's style you are critical of. If, on the other hand, you say you never thought anyone could interest you in a novel about an economics professor, but the book was so *readable* that it was a pleasure, that's style you are talking about, too.

Novelist Irene Hunt said it better: "Style is the outpouring of the writer's self—his perceptions of life, his grace or lack of grace, his courage or his whining self-pity, his humility and compassion, his arrogance and cynicism."

Letting it come

Style is the one thing writers need not think much about when beginning to write a novel, because the book will naturally reflect each author's unique characteristics. If the story comes from the heart—the gut, if you will—style will creep into the way you write almost without your being conscious of it. In searching for the right way to tell the story—via mood, plot, characters, and theme—as you try different approaches, different voices, you will at last settle into a manner of writing that suits both you and the story. That will be your style.

Nor should readers be too conscious of style while reading your novel, certainly not as an element apart from all others. If the book is well written, readers will be engrossed in the characters and their dilemmas; they will not be distracted by the author's use of little-known words or his attitudes toward women (at least not until they have finished the book). They will not, in other words, be aware of the author on every page.

In describing the novel to others, however, readers may call it clever or humorous or low-key or dramatic; they might also call it pedantic, erudite, repetitive, or sluggish. They are describing the voice of the author—the style.

Some experienced authors do pay a great deal of attention to style, and are known as stylists. But the basis for every novel should be the story and characters. If there is nothing on which to build a marvelous exhibition, then style is like the latest Paris fashion which, though decorative and eye-catching, may be decidedly uncomfortable and impractical, and no one would want to wear it for very long.

Developing your style

To allow yourself the freedom and the atmosphere in which your style can develop naturally as you write, don't pay too much attention to grammatical rules. Certainly not in the first draft of the first chapter. Let the words come, let them flow, toss them in the air, so to speak, and see in what patterns and shapes they land. Play with them. Read them aloud as you write them down, so that you are hearing the words as they form phrases and sentences. Sometimes hearing the sound of them together propels you forward, making you aware of the lilt, the rhythm, the humor, the pathos, the drama or the wit that is inherent in them.

Worrying about grammar at this point can take the life out of the writing, make it sound stilted, formal—and rob the author of his own voice.

Oftentimes the right style for a particular novel won't be obvious to you until the third or fourth chapter, or you may be oblivious to it altogether. It is not unusual for critics and readers to praise or damn a writer's style, while the writer may have little idea of what they are talking about. He was so intent on his characters, on the story he had to tell, on the theme that had been eating away at him, that he simply "told the story in the way that seemed best." When he hears others analyzing his style, it is as though it is someone else's book they are talking about.

Nor is a writer's style likely to be the same from novel to novel. It could be, but if the author is prolific, and especially if he attempts many different types of subjects and themes, his books may—and should—have a variety of styles. "Morbid" or "witty" or "a tendency toward pedantic narration" does not mean that this is the whole sum of a writer's style. It may be typical of the author's voice in one particular book, but it says nothing at all about the books to come. Just as a friend may be carefree on one occasion and serious on another, optimistic over some circumstance in his life or cynical about another, so may an author change his style from book to book.

While critics and teachers of creative writing may be focusing on an author's style, the writer—at work on the next novel and the next—will be focusing on structure and technique, which take conscious, purposeful effort, and do not sneak into a novel as style seems to.

Choices

In deciding on structure and technique, you have many choices, probably all of them used before, but perhaps not quite in the same way that you will use them for *this* novel. To help you make a sound decision, ask yourself some of the questions you asked regarding the choice of viewpoint. Will you tell the story from the eyes of several characters or of only one? If so, will each character get his own chapter, a part of a chapter, paragraphs within the chapter, or an entire section of the book? Will it be third person, first person? Will it be stream-of-consciousness? Will the events take place in straight chronological order, or will there be flashbacks?

Should the book start and end with the same scene, with all the action told in the flashbacks? Will there be a sequel, and if so, should some of the material be reserved for later?

Your choice of structure and technique will depend not just on a whim, but on the characters themselves, the plot, the theme, and the type of fiction you are writing. Do you want the events of the story to move quickly, uninterrupted by flashbacks? In scenes of intense, dramatic activity, sentences will probably, and appropriately, be kept short, so that they read in a rapid-fire manner:

> Doug stood motionless inside the door. The footsteps in the other room stopped. He could hear the tick of the clock. A drip from the kitchen sink. Outside, the noise of traffic kept a steady hum. But here in the apartment, someone was waiting in the other room. Doug waited too.

He edged, at last, along the wall. Past the desk, the chair. A floorboard creaked. The silence in the other room seemed a living thing. The intruder's breath was almost audible. Doug heard nothing more, but knew that someone was still there.

If you are writing a mystery novel, you must leave clues along the way, for readers must be able, if they are perceptive enough, to pick up the proper clues and come to the right conclusions. If the book is to be a gothic tale, mood must positively ooze from the pages. If it is romance, make readers experience sensuality in your descriptions of the clothes, the sheets, the grass, the wine.

When writing about a three-generational family, you should ask if the story would make more sense if it began with the parents' lives, following them through their youth and middle years before focusing on their children.

Do you want to start the book with a bang—with the climax—and work backward, so that the focal point will not be on what happened as much as on *how* it happened or why?

Should this thriller have many climaxes, so that each time the drum beat grows louder and the mood music swells, readers wonder, hearts pounding, "Is this it?" How gratified they will be to discover that, terrifying as this scene was, the "biggie" is yet to come.

Influences on style and structure

How a book is structured depends not only on the characters and the story, but sometimes on new discoveries you make along the way, possibly as you research the background for the book.

Let us suppose that an author, with a particular plot and characters in mind but no particular setting, travels through a section of Pennsylvania, and is fascinated by some of the old Mennonite farms. He decides that he would like to set his story there, and in researching homes of the area, discovers that some were built over springs, so that the water actually bubbled up out of the dirt floor in the cellar and ran out through an opening in one wall. This suggests possible changes in plot, in mood, in structure.

Such a house would undoubtedly be damp, and the elderly inhabitants might suffer from rheumatism and other ailments. In a historical novel, this house would be a potential fortress in case of attack, having its own water supply. A house with a spring in the cellar could also be the scene of a child's accidental drowning. After a tragedy like this, the occupants might have tried to block off the spring, but perhaps it kept cropping up in another area. There could even be intimations of the occult; there could be ghosts of ages past, their faces appearing in the water. The water might be poisoned; the spring could dry up or prove to have some magical powers, with omens of things to come . . . .

With such a discovery, does the author want to stick with his original plot and theme and structure, consigning the presence of a spring in the cellar to that large stack of known facts that will *not* play a part in the story? Or does he want somehow to incorporate this new material? Will he want to start the story with a generation that lived in the house earlier, in another era, and if so, should the book be divided into sections rather than chapters, each focusing on a different generation and what part the spring played in their lives?

Only a small amount of all the information gleaned in research is used in a novel. This does not mean that the information was not valuable. Whatever the author keeps in mind during the writing will help him determine what is to be said, yet very little may appear on the printed page.

The author's imprint

It is not the author's style alone or structure or technique that leaves an identifying mark on a book but rather the sum of all the elements: the characters and the manner in which they are portrayed, the tightness or looseness of the plot, the dialogue and the cryptic way in which it is written or the leisurely manner in which the characters relate to each other. It may reveal itself in the author's own insight into life and the human condition, or in his use of original, inventive phrases.

A novelist's imprint on a book depends also on its theme. Reviewers often cite certain writers who seem to have one main theme that they use again and again in their novels— but in endless variation. There is nothing wrong with this, and in any case, it is often done unconsciously. Exploring the different facets of a theme may be fascinating not only to the author but to readers as well.

Other authors may choose a different theme for every novel. Some use the same characters from book to book. And then there are authors who take only a character or two from one book to the next, possibly assigning them a principal role in one, a cameo performance in another. Some select the same city or region or state for all their stories.

There are authors who write only mysteries, some only science fiction; some may always center their stories on the rich and famous, some on the working class. Novels have been written that are pre-quels—set in a time period prior to a related novel, already published, by the same author. Some writers are known for the symbolism in their works, or for long philosophic discourses. There are novels that are so much a part of the author's psyche that he feels compelled to share these events and experiences with his readers.

No hard-and-fast rules exist about what can be done

stylistically or structurally or thematically, other than that a good novel should be written with taste and clarity and purpose. If an author skips from one viewpoint to another so often that readers have barely begun to know one character before they are asked to meet another, the spell of the story is broken. If an author uses words—pedantic or vulgar or words known only to a certain group of people—to the point that they intrude upon the story, then readers are more conscious of the words than of the characters and their feelings, and the writer may have overdone it and spoiled the impact of the novel.

The most important thing is the story and the characters who make it move. Nothing should detract from them; nothing should overshadow them; nothing should make readers aware of the author behind the scenes.

𝕊 12

When the Writing Goes Flat

WHEN YOU BEGIN A MANUSCRIPT with a great burst of enthusiasm and discover, in chapter three, that all the life has gone out of the writing, that the characters are just moving about mechanically on stage, that *your* interest has dwindled, it is somewhat akin to finding that your beautiful new car has a flat. Except that in the case of a car, you know what to do or whom to call.

You felt so sure of this one, you couldn't wait to get up in the morning to begin the writing. The first line couldn't have been better—the first page, the whole first chapter, practically. You read it aloud to yourself. You loved it. It wasn't perfect, of course, but there were enough wonderful parts to it that you knew you could edit and revise the rest into shape. And now, suddenly, looking down at the paper before you, you realize that for the last six pages you have simply been spinning your wheels. Your plot is going nowhere, and the characters don't seem to help.

Every novelist who has ever lived has felt this way, most of us many, many times. Nobody put it better than Flannery O'Connor: "Writing a novel is a terrible experience, during which the hair often falls out and the teeth decay."

Philip Roth said: *"The Anatomy Lesson* went through a crisis like every book I've ever written. About a year into it, it seems to me ghastly. And it *is* ghastly. Dead. And then I've got to sit and look at it every day—six months of a difficult time." He says he throws out scenes and characters until he's left with "all the pieces that are alive. And I say, 'What connects these living things? What is the real pattern of this book as opposed to the one I imposed upon it to get it going?'"

As he has shown, being in a rut is not the same as falling into a well and not being able to hoist yourself back up. There are strategies that work, not all of them all of the time, but at least some of them some of the time. And each writer eventually discovers what helps him most.

Keeping quiet

A great many writers find it necessary to keep that first burst of enthusiasm throughout the writing of the novel, and they do this by not talking about what they are working on. For some writers this isn't important; they discuss their "work in progress" incessantly with whoever will listen. Outsiders often think that writers who won't talk about their work are afraid their ideas will be stolen, but it's usually something very different: Talking about a plot often diminishes the emotion, just as talking out a problem relieves anger and stress.

Most of us begin each book with the assumption—the hope, anyway—that it will be better than the one before. We're wild about it before we even start. We're in love. We see only the pluses and none of the problems that this particular plot or those particular characters are going to cause us. That's what drives us to our desks in the morning and makes us want to write everything down quickly, quickly, before it gets away.

If we start talking to others about our story—even a one-line description of the plot—there is no reaction they can give that matches our own feeling about the book, unless they clasp their hands together and breathe, "Oh, that's wonderful! How did you ever think of such a magnificent story?" Nobody ever reacts that way. If they are charitable, they smile and say, "Hm, that could be interesting!" but more often than not, they say, somewhat tentatively, "Hasn't that been done before?" or "What do you know about coal miners?" or "Do you really think it would sell?"

That is not what a writer needs to hear. And because we dare not let anyone burst our bubble, we should keep our ideas to ourselves.

Troubleshooting

Yet, having kept the secret, you can still feel life oozing out of your project. There are writers who claim that the best way to keep a story alive is always to stop in the middle of a terrific scene, so that they can pick it up again the next day and move ahead on this momentum. There is something to be said for that, although if you find the words flowing fast and everything in sync, it seems hard to justify stopping the flow.

It sometimes works best to start out writing each day with the understanding that the very moment you find the writing going flat, you will stop, put the manuscript aside, and come back to it that afternoon or the next day or even a week later. You may be amazed at the amount of perspective you gain just by going for a 30-minute walk, running an errand, chopping wood. It gets you out of the story temporarily, and you may find when you come back to it again that you see clearly where you went astray and what needs to be done to correct the problem.

But let's say that you don't see clearly. The next thing to do is to read backwards, so to speak, to find the place where the scene began to go flat. Was it the beginning of that scene? That chapter? Was it where a certain character entered the room? Was it where the dialogue stopped and you had to write a few transitional paragraphs? Finding where the action or dialogue lagged is half the problem. If, of course, you have to go all the way back to the beginning and find that you don't like the whole thing as much as you thought, then you need to rethink the project and ask yourself some questions:

Did you choose to write this particular novel because it genuinely stirred something inside you, made you feel you had a lot to say, and had the characters to bring it to life?

Or did you choose this story because a similar type of novel made the best-seller list? Because it's about your grandmother, and you want it published before she dies? Because you want your children to know how much you care for them, and your character Amy is the epitome of your daughter? Because this topic seems to be "in" these days? Because you were going to India anyway, so if you wrote a book in that setting, you could claim a tax deduction? Because you desperately need the money an advance would bring? Because you want to get back at all the lawyers you had to deal with when you got your divorce?

And finally, the most basic question of all: Do you want to write even more than you want to be A Writer? Is the attraction the putting of words on paper, or is it the idea of living a writer's life that appeals? Some people would prefer to stand around at cocktail parties *talking* about writing more than they want to write. They want their names on a published book; they just don't want to have to do the work. You might as well be honest with yourself, because if you aren't, your editor will be.

Let's say, however, that none of these questions applies to you, and though you can tell that something is wrong, you just *know* that the novel as a whole is not wrong. Something just seems out of whack. In this case, ask yourself if the story would move better if it were told in first person rather than third person. Would this help bring your character to life? Is there something about the way he or she speaks that would help the novel ring true? Would first-person make the story more humorous? Give it more local flavor?

On the other hand, are you writing in the first person about a character who would not be the kind to reveal too much about himself, certainly not about what he is feeling? If you switched to third person, or even the omniscient point of view, would this put the novel on the right track?

Is it the beginning itself that's wrong? Does it set the reader up for a different kind of story from the one you have to tell? If you were the reader, after reading the first page or paragraph, would you want to stick with it? Have you told just enough to pique your reader's interest, but not so much that you've given the plot away?

Transitions

If the novel started out well, however, and you have found the place it went flat, then you have to do some detective work. What changed at that point in the story that made a paragraph different from the one before? If it doesn't seem to be working, how could you do it differently?

Instead of the long scene about what happened over the weekend, getting your character from Friday to Monday, could you sum it up in a few sentences, such as "On Saturday, she said her goodbyes. On Sunday she left. And when the train pulled in on Monday, she. . . ." or simply, "When the train pulled in on Monday. . ."

Too often we forget that we are not writing a diary. We do not have to record everything a character says or feels or does. We need only hit the highlights, need only tell enough to enable the readers to see the character and understand his motivation clearly. By backing up to the part of the manuscript that was going well and then taking a running leap once again, we can often hurl ourselves into that tough paragraph in a different manner, see it from another point of view, think of an entirely new way to present it, or even decide we don't need it at all.

We often have notions that have no reality whatever. We sometimes feel that if a story takes place between October and Christmas, we must automatically tell what the character was doing on Thanksgiving, whether it is significant or relevant to the story or not, only because we think the readers will want to know; because Thanksgiving is important in our house; because we still remember how we celebrated every holiday when we were in school. We may need to discard ideas we have carried around since childhood. If it is Sunday in our story, for example, we do not have to say whether or not our characters went to church, unless this is important in the novel.

We can see a family eating without knowing what exactly they are putting in their mouths; we can say a few brief lines about how a family celebrated Christmas without knowing what gifts were exchanged. We can show a man taking a woman out for the evening without detailing everything that went on from the time he picked her up until he brought her home again.

If what they did is not important to the story, but his increasing irritation with her is, it may be enough to say, "He did not like the way she tapped her foot on the floor of the car; he did not like the way she interrogated the waiter about the broccoli soup; and he especially did not like the way she murmured little questions aloud all during the movie." Only you can decide whether this evening warranted more about the woman in question, or whether she, or the evening with her, could be dismissed with a few phrases.

At the other extreme, your transitions may be too abrupt, with not enough detail. This can be especially true when you introduce new characters. As a general rule, it's a good idea to bring them into the novel slowly, at intervals, not all on the same page. A garden party or a family dinner or an ambassador's reception may, in the final analysis, be the way you want to open your book, but be aware that your readers are meeting all these people for the first time. Think of going to a party and being introduced to all the guests in rapid succession. You try desperately to remember their names, to match husbands and wives, and put last names and first names together—and it can be very confusing.

Give each character a distinctive enough trademark so readers will have a mental image of him when he enters the novel. It might be age, a limp, dialect, personality, or dress. You must do this very subtly, of course, so you do not have a circus with each performer doing his specialty.

When there are several characters in your first scene, avoid introducing by name any whom the reader does not have to know that very minute. If your reader has to keep turning back to page one to remember who Leila was, and who was married to the trumpet player, you are breaking the rhythm of your story unnecessarily.

Getting the most from a scene

Sometimes a scene doesn't work because we are trying to make it do too much, like a donkey with too many packs on its back. If you are not only trying to tell how Edward Halstead worked his way up to be vice-president of Mercantile, Incorporated, but also trying to let the reader know his dreams for his son, his son's dreams, his son's wife's dreams, and the lust Edward feels for his secretary, you are overburdening the scene and lessening its effect.

On the other hand, a scene may not work because it doesn't do enough. A lighthearted conversation between a young man and a young woman, meeting perhaps for the first time, may be so light and frothy that there's simply no substance or point to it.

We are not making enough of the scene. It's all right to show the two characters afraid to say anything beyond the banal remarks one might make on a first date, but we need to give some insight into what they are thinking, some revelation of their personalities. Is he shy? Is she thinking that he probably finds her boring? Is he afraid to risk talking about something that really interests him, and as a consequence, are they likely to lose each other because they never allow themselves to *be* themselves?

A scene may not work because it does not have enough variety. Perhaps it is written totally in narration when it desperately needs a change of pace, a few lines of dialogue. Or you might, instead, have pages and pages of dialogue, the characters nattering on and on, when the reader would like a little respite, some silence, while the characters quietly sip their wine and mull over what was said. You may have kept a single setting too long: the preceding four scenes all took place in the country, and readers are eager to find out what's happening to Charlene after she got to Chicago.

Plain old bad writing

Sometimes the writing goes flat simply because of bad writing. Possibly you were tired and lapsed into clichés without realizing it; or you used trite or hackneyed situations and phrases. Maybe you changed viewpoint, and instead of looking outward from your character's eyes, you find that you were writing *about* him instead.

Did you use stilted dialogue or pet words that jar, or include a particular word too many times on a page, use too many adjectives or adverbs, or overuse dialect? Your writing might have fallen flat because it is grammatically too correct, your English so precise that it doesn't bend at all and your characters seem stiff. Perhaps the speech idiom of your protagonist does not match his thought idiom. Your transitions might be jerky.

This is a good place to remind yourself that you must not *tell* the story so much as you must *show* it. One does not say, *Karen was so upset with Mack that she could scarcely speak. Everything he said only seemed to make things worse. At last she stormed from the room and went upstairs.*

Instead, show Karen entering the room. Describe the tension in her face, her body, her hands. Let readers hear what she first says to Mack; let them hear his reply, her response. Build up the tension until at last Karen has had enough; describe how she turns and rushes from the room, what she is feeling, and what she does once she is upstairs.

Maybe your writing doesn't read well because you have included more details than necessary, crowding the pages and slowing the action. "Perhaps for a novelist it's detrimental to read too much," said William Styron. "I've always had a fear of cluttering my mind with too much detail, when the point of the novel is to be able to make leaps into the imagination."

If you suspect that your page or chapter went flat because of bad writing but aren't sure, read a few chapters from novels you *know* are good; then go back to your own. Sometimes there's no better way than this to shape up.

The value of lapsed time

It is easier to find the source of the problem when all of it is located in one character, one scene, one conversation—far, far more difficult when a manuscript is full of good scenes and good characters but somehow, as a whole, misses its mark. The sum of the parts, for example, may not equal the whole that you had in mind when you began; may not illustrate the particular theme you set out to illuminate; may not make the readers feel the way you wanted them to feel at the end; may not, in essence, do the job.

When you can't put your finger on what's wrong, but you or the editors who have seen it simply know it's not right—when what is wrong is so elusive it can't quite be put into words—it is better to put the manuscript aside temporarily and go on to something else. Give yourself a few months or even a year of working on something completely different. And then on a day you feel fresh and energetic and in an objective frame of mind, get out that original manuscript and read it once again. It is quite possible that the trouble will leap out at you like a beast from a closet.

How could I have made my main character so disagreeable? you might ask yourself. I *thought* I'd liked the guy! What a depressing setting! What a downer of a plot! Where's the humor? Where's the conflict? Where's the poignancy? It's so sentimental! It's so contrived! How would I ever have thought I could have James Bannister drive so recklessly when he has never taken a chance in his life? Have I led up to this scene? Have I properly motivated him? Since I love this scene and the conclusion, how would the plot have to be changed to make this ending believable?

As a matter of fact, it is an excellent idea always, with *every* manuscript, to put it aside for weeks or even months before making your final revisions and sending it in. One publisher has said that if every author, upon completion of his manuscript, put it away for a year and then gave it a final rewrite, there would be far more manuscripts accepted. You may want to put it away and go back to it several times, not just once. Do this as long as you find major changes to make—more than just a word here and there. If you see the days or the weeks slipping away and are fearful that the novel will take forever, remember that editors look more favorably on a manuscript that needs only a little editing than those that need a complete overhaul.

But nothing will help you be more objective than the lapse of time. And nothing will help you correct what is wrong in a manuscript as much as seeing for yourself what it was that didn't work.

The art of self-criticism

One of the most arduous things writers must learn is to critique their own work. This process is often as difficult and painful for the published writer as it is for the novice.

Asking someone else to read and give you an opinion of your manuscript can be either disastrous, not useful, or exceedingly helpful, depending on how able and objective he or she is and how you respond to criticism. Sometimes another person can tell you exactly what's wrong but the suggestions as to how to fix it miss the mark. At other times someone may know where in the manuscript something is not right, but not know what it is or how to improve it.

Whether or not someone else gives an opinion, you yourself must make the revisions and decisions. Your greatest mistake would be to send in a manuscript that is not the best it can be, not as good as you know you are capable of. All too often, if most of the manuscript reads well, we overlook the "gray" areas—those sentences or paragraphs that don't seem quite right even yet, but which we think no one will notice. Someone will notice.

Self-criticism is important even if, when you've finished your manuscript, you really like it. You may even love it. You want to be sure, however, that it is as close to perfect as you can get before you send it to the editor. What else do you need to ask yourself before you type up the final draft?

1. What was it I wanted to do in this novel, and how well did I do it?

2. Is there unity and coherence in the manuscript? Do things come around full circle?

3. Does the story "flow"?

4. Is the logic sound?

5. Have I given the main theme, main plot, and main character enough emphasis?

6. How do the words look there on paper? Are the paragraphs nicely broken up with dialogue in places, or are there too many pages of narrative in succession?

7. Do the dates and ages and times check out?

It is quite amazing sometimes the details the writer overlooks in working hard to get other things right. A letter from my editor regarding *Alice in Rapture, Sort Of* contained this paragraph:

> At the start, one must assume that that first day is sometime during at least the second week of vacation. The sleepover could be the Friday of the second week of vacation. But that would make it near the end of June already. Patrick's birthday then has to come during the third week of vacation—are we getting into July? A week later the permanent has to be in the 4th week of vacation—surely well into July. Yet on page 67 there are still two months of vacation left and on 82 it is still the middle of July and a lot seems to have happened in between. On page 92 it is still the middle of July. But then on 93 it is the first week of August. The rest seems pretty much OK, though

they are gone the first week in August, come back to a week of rain, and then we have some sequences of events that could not have happened in the rain and it is still the middle of August.

Dealing with rejection

You may think that the really good writers, the famous writers, work hard on a manuscript, revise it several times, turn it in, and it's accepted. Not quite. One very successful author, whose many books have received great critical acclaim, had a manuscript returned by her agent who said it was "not up to her previous work." So the writer threw it out. All that work! we think. All that time! It happens.

Even if you have worked very long and hard on a manuscript and finally have to put it aside, there is a possibility you may revive it later and turn it into something publishable. Or you may take a character or two from it, or a scene, or the theme, or whole chapters, in fact, and make of them something new.

But even if the novel is never published, you can learn a great deal from the experience. Writing that novel may have been something you simply had to get out of your system before you could go on to another. It may be that you were trying to accomplish something that was just not for you and, having tried it, you can turn your attention to a more suitable plot. It is possible, too, that it took so long to write your novel that by the time you finished, the theme or the plot were outdated and, realizing that, you can accept the rejection more readily.

Sometimes it is not your writing that goes flat but your confidence. Perhaps, while working on your novel, you receive a rejection slip—a form letter rejection!—for something else. No helpful hints, no condolences, no offer to look at other manuscripts you may have written. (I used to receive a printed card that said only, "Sorry.")

First, remember that only one particular piece of your writing is being rejected, not you as a person or your whole career. Editors reject novels for all sorts of reasons, and sometimes they even reject good ones because it is a type of novel their house doesn't usually publish, and they know that they wouldn't have much success marketing it. But suppose that this isn't just a form letter, but the worst kind of rejection slip. A form letter with a message scribbled at the end of it that says, in this editor's opinion, your manuscript is not salable—that it is trite and poorly written. Or suppose you are a published author, and a review of your new book says much the same thing. How do you deal with despair?

You are human, of course, and you are certainly allowed a few hours of anguish over a discouraging letter or review. John Updike has said that, on reading an unfavorable review of one of his novels, "My ears close up, my eyes go warm, my chest feels thin as an eggshell, my voice churns silently in my stomach." Ah, yes.

All right, so it hurts. But it is not a death sentence. It does not say that you will never write a good novel as long as you live. As novelists—observers and listeners—we, of all people, should trust our ability to grow and change. A writer can produce a very ordinary novel one year—even a bad one—yet come up with a novel a year or so later that the critics will pronounce profound.

Sometimes we just haven't found the type of writing that best fits our talents: We are attempting what we feel we *should* write, or what we think will sell, rather than the story that we can tell best.

The most important question to ask yourself after a disappointment of this kind is, "What can I learn from it?" You do not call the editor and argue with him. You do not write the reviewer a nasty letter. There is only one thing you can really do about it, only one thing you *should* do: Write a better book. Write a book so wonderful that the editor will want to do everything possible to get it published.

Remember that in the careers of writers there are often stories of a huge success after several dismal failures. Also, sometimes the writer whose first book is a great success "peaks" too early and never writes another novel, at least not another one as good. What has happened in your writing career before may have little bearing on your next book. Every novel is a whole new ballgame, and there is every chance that the next time you may succeed.

☜ 13

What You Can Teach Yourself

THE EXCITING THING ABOUT WRITING is that you can produce a good, even great, novel without ever having taken a creative writing course, read any books about writing, or majored in English literature in college. You don't have to have a degree in anything or be of a particular age to be a published author. The words you put down on paper, the way you arrange them, and the feelings they evoke can move an editor to publish your book.

There is much we can teach ourselves about writing, because everything we do or see or hear or are can be used, somehow, in a novel. We are constantly seeing characters in people we meet, deducing their motives, sensing plots, thinking up resolutions. Jerzy Kosinski once said: "Writing is the essence of my life—whatever else I do revolves around a constant thought: could I—can I—would I—should I—use it in my next novel?"

Improving description

You can make yourself a better writer of description by consciously focusing on choosing adjectives, creating metaphors and similes. When going for a daily walk, for example, you can consciously observe everything along the way more closely than you usually do. You won't let yourself get away simply with observing that the buds on a box elder are little tufts of brownish-red, but you will try to see in your mind's eye exactly what they look like, and you will think, at last, that they have the shape of splayed bristles on an old toothbrush.

The snow on a busy street has the appearance of brown sugar; the water on the lake shines like the steel blade of a knife. Try to see a thing for more than it is, for something that will help give your reader a stronger mental image than the "shiny surface of the lake" or the "red buds of the box elder."

Improving dialogue

You can make yourself a better writer of dialogue by consciously becoming a more dedicated eavesdropper. You can become expert at this while giving the appearance of being contemplative or even asleep. Children will reveal the most amazing things about themselves to their friends if the adult in the next room will just keep quiet. If you do not interrupt their conversation or interject tidbits of wisdom here and there, but simply go on rummaging through a drawer or crinkling a newspaper, children will assume you are not only hard at work but deaf as well.

If you read a book in a restaurant when you are eating alone, even if you are only staring at the pages and turn one at intervals, the people at the next table will be more likely to talk uninhibitedly. And while you do not listen at bedroom doors or in on private phone conversations, there is nothing to say that you must wear earplugs to keep from overhearing what people say at a party or in public.

Improving characterization

Henry James once said, "Be one of those upon whom nothing is lost."

If you have difficulty describing what characters in your novel do as they talk—little mannerisms they use which would help you break up the dialogue—pay close attention the next time you attend a party. Be a camera. What posture do people take when they're sitting in a chair? What do they do with their bodies—their hands, their feet, their shoulders? Do they talk in complete sentences? Interrupt each other frequently? Finish sentences for each other? How do they express concern? Shock? Indignation? Envy? What facial expressions give them away? Note any changes in the voice of a person expressing disappointment.

To increase your power of observation further, you can give yourself specific exercises to do. For example, write a description of your hand. Give yourself five minutes, and take the full five. In all likelihood, you will discover something about your hand you had never really noticed before: the length of the fingers in relation to each other; the half-moon on your nails, or the absence of it; lines in the fingernail; the size of your knuckles; what about your veins, freckles, or age spots? The little wrinkles on the backs of your fingers, or the way each side of your fingernail meets the skin?

If you have trouble becoming your characters, try this exercise:

In one paragraph, write a description of the room you are in from the viewpoint of a six-year-old child; a 16-year-old boy; a 46-year-old woman; a 76-year-old man.

It is the same room, but each of those people would see it differently. The six-year-old would probably notice the candy in the dish, the red fringe on the curtains, the clock in the shape of a cat. The 16-year-old would notice the candy dish, too, but would also glance casually through the magazines on the coffee table to see if there was a copy of *Glamour, People,* or *Sports Illustrated.* The 46-year-old woman would see the oiled teak table, the hanging fern, and would sit where she could keep one eye on the six-year-old. The elderly man would notice at once whether the room was too hot or too cold, and might look around for a straight-backed chair.

But watch out, because it is easy to generalize and stereotype. The child, walking into a room, may notice the less obvious things as well: the formal way the men and women are talking, the trivial subjects they are talking about, the distance between them as they sit, the subtle ways they contradict each other. An adult, by the same token, could very well walk into that same room and see only the superficial: the clothes and jewelry that people are wearing, the porcelain tea cups, a man's toupee.

The 76-year-old man could have sat down in his straight-backed chair and given his attention and admiration to the young hostess. Don't necessarily assume that an elderly man would tune in a nature program on TV; he might very well want to watch the Miss America pageant.

To gain another perspective on becoming characters of different ages, imagine a situation in which a teen-age girl, her mother, and her three-year-old brother are on a shopping trip. The mother leaves the child in the care of his older sister, and goes off to the linen department. When she returns, her agitated daughter tells her that a friend came along, she got distracted, and the little brother has wandered off.

What is the mother feeling at this point? What are the physical sensations she experiences? What does she say? What does she do?

Do the same for the girl and her younger brother. Describe the panic of the three-year-old who wandered off to look at the escalator, and when he tried to return, found that his sister wasn't there. Can you take yourself back to a time you were separated from a parent in a department store—that terrifying sense of aloneness when you looked up and saw only strangers? And will you remember, as you write your paragraph, that the child would be looking up? That looking straight ahead he sees only the legs, not the faces, of strangers around him?

What are his physical feelings—the tightness in the chest, a rush of blood to the head, pupils dilating, breath coming short?

What is the child thinking? That he may never find his mother and sister again? That they have deserted him? That a stranger will carry him off? That the store will close, and no one will come for him, and he'll be locked inside?

What does he do? Fight for control—pretend at first that everything is O.K.? Does he struggle to hold back tears and finally give in to silent crying? Does he cringe as people look at him, and find himself unable to answer when a woman asks what is wrong? Can you describe his relief at having a sales clerk take over?

Portray the scene when the child and mother are reunited. How many times have you seen a mother—now that the terror is past—react with anger, shaking the child and instructing him never to wander off again?

Observe yourself as well as others. How do you sit when you're bored? Do you have a mannerism while eating that you could impart to one of your characters—something that would help bring him to life on paper? Do you, for example, eat all of your vegetables before you start on your meat? Do you eat everything counterclockwise on your plate?

What sound do new jeans make when you walk? What do they feel like when you put them on? Take a good look at your room. What do you almost never hang up? What sounds do you hear in your kitchen? If you were to lie on your back on your sofa and stare at the ceiling, what would

you see? Small cracks? Spots? What shape are they? Do you
see light and shadow from a window? Lights of cars going
by at night, crossing the ceiling? Can you identify sounds
you hear when you wake up? From inside the house? From
outside? Be a recorder.

But are these little details really important? you might
ask. Yes, because they help the reader feel that he is there.
"Fred lay on his bed and worried about Sharon," does not
convey what Fred is feeling nearly as well as "Fred lay on
his bed and stared at the ceiling, thinking about Sharon.
Fine cracks in the plaster radiated out from the light fix-
ture in several directions, like the worry pains in his chest,
traveling down his arms and legs."

What does a bookstore smell like? What does your minister do when the offering is being taken? Stare out the
window? Sit with chin in hands? Tap his foot? How can you
tell when your wife is worried about something? Describe
your mother's face when she is angry. Describe your
brother's laugh, your son's sneakers, the look of the dog's
dish after he has finished eating, the shed in your back
yard.

Branching out

How do other writers describe people, objects, and feelings? How do actors express their emotions? Always ask
yourself "what if?" What if the writer had done it this way
or that way? What effect would it likely have had on the plot
or the characters? What if the actor had been standing
when he said his last line? Would that have made a difference? What if the ending had been thus and so? What
then?

Familiarize yourself not only with the work of other
writers, but with other types of fiction and novels for different age levels. A high percentage of the American public
believes that if you can write fiction for adults, then ob-

viously you can write successful fiction for children as well. This idea must come from the mistaken assumption that just as one grows from infancy to adulthood, a writer begins with picture books and works up to the adult level. Not so. Many writers of adult literature write terrible books for children. And of those who write for all ages, some would say that a picture book—an excellent picture book—is most difficult of all, because, like poetry, every word has to be in exactly the right order. It can be as difficult to write simply, to condense, to distill, as it is to elaborate.

Some writers think that novels for young adults offer more freedom than any other type, for not only can the subject matter be almost as sophisticated and varied as in a novel for adults, not only can plots and subplots be complex and bold and dramatic, but there is also more tolerance for the quiet novel of substance. There is far less concern about whether such a novel will become a best seller and more emphasis, instead, on quality.

To my knowledge, there is not a single theme that cannot be written about in a children's or young adult novel, if it is handled with sensitivity and taste. There are now on the market children's and young adult novels dealing with divorce, infidelity, obesity, homosexuality, menstruation, death, violence, income tax evasion, sexual intercourse, terrorism, murder, nuclear war, persecution, prejudice, masturbation, informers, prisons, war criminals, and torture. Each of these subjects, of course, is presented from a child's or a teen-ager's point of view, and the situations either involve or are of vital concern to a child or teen-ager.

Familiarize yourself with fiction for children and young adults to get acquainted with their worlds, their way of thinking, and how life appears to them. You may be surprised at the range and depth of the material, themes, subjects, and subtleties.

Consider the three excerpts below, each taken from a

novel. See if you can deduce which of them are from adult novels and which of them are for children:

1. I studied the German soldier nearest us, trying to think of something that might make him uneasy, or frightened, but nothing came. The flat, unsmiling face, the glinting bayonet, and the polished boots all seemed impervious to thought, let alone fear. There is, as I later found out, no real fear unless you think about it; there is sudden terror, but that is more easily controlled than the kind of fear that gnaws away over a period of time. The first thing we had to do was make these people think. I use the word "people" loosely, because except for the one I saw briefly smiling, they were as impersonal as tanks.

Ole had been studying the same soldier, and after a while he said, "You know what? The son of a bitch likes it."

"Likes what?" I asked.

"The attention. He's never had so many people looking at him."

2. The daughter of a samurai does not cry out in childbirth. Within her head Takiko laughed at the injunction. It was as though her very body was the koto of a god whose powerful hand struck a chord so fierce that for the wild moment she became the storm music of the sea. Then throbbing, ebbing, the great wave would pass over her, and she would drift on the surface of the water, the sun warm upon her face until another stroke upon the strings.

I am mixing it all up, she smiled. *I am music and storm and strings. I am Izanami as She brooded over Creation.*

The storm built with a deafening crescendo until her flesh could no longer contain it. Takiko cried out—a cry of triumph and joy. Who could keep silent at such a victory?

Then she heard a tiny angry squall.

"It is a girl," the peasant midwife observed dully.

3. In the kitchen, a cupboard door bangs.

"I'll go check on the popcorn," he says.

She has her back to him, all business.

"Jen, what's the matter?"

"Nothing. Never mind. I'm acting dopey tonight. Just forget it, ignore it, okay?"

"Okay," he says. "He seemed like a nice enough guy to me."

"Well, he's not!" she snaps. "A man who dates a married woman, in my opinion, is not a nice guy."

"I thought your parents were divorced."

"They are! Now they are! They weren't before he came along. He was a friend of my father's—" She stops abruptly. "I'm sorry, this is all very boring for you."

"I'm not bored."

"Well, you should be. I am. And I don't like acting like this over it. And especially I don't like it, in front of you."

"Why, in front of me?"

He moves across the kitchen, toward her, and she quickly turns her head away. She is crying. "Oh, damn!" she says. "I'm sorry, I can't help it, oh, damn."

The three books were, in order, *Bright Candles: A Novel of the Danish Resistance,* by Nathaniel Benchley; *Of Nightingales that Weep,* by Katherine Paterson; and *Ordinary People,* by Judith Guest, only the last one for adults.

Tricks of the trade

If you are a published writer, you may learn a good deal by rereading all the reviews of your novels. Whether published or unpublished, the letters you have received from editors are equally informative. On one sheet of paper write all the negative comments; on another, the positive. Then try to find a common thread. What type of criticism did you get again and again? What elements were praised? How can you change your writing in the future to make use of what you do best and steer away from the things that just haven't seemed to work?

Take a manuscript of yours and choose a particularly undistinguished passage. It may be a transition section, getting your character from Paris to Vienna, or from May to June. Or select another section of the manuscript in which some note must be made of what is happening, but only as a bridge between a more interesting scene that precedes it and the one that follows. Try to bring the weak paragraphs to life. Forget the scenes before and after, and concentrate only on this one section. Pretend that all you have to do that day is to bring sparkle and grace to these lines. You may be surprised at the results when you concentrate on a paragraph and give it your best.

See if you are growing as a writer by reading things you wrote three to five years ago, published as well as unpublished. If you find in almost every story, article, or novel some paragraphs, sentences, or even a word that you would change now, scenes you could improve upon, characters you would portray more sharply, you are growing.

You can teach yourself patience. If you can't bring yourself to put a finished manuscript away for a year to give yourself perspective when you look at it again, try six months. Four months. Three weeks.

If you waste a day because you wrote nothing worth saving, don't worry about it. It comes with the territory.

Don't hesitate to start a novel over, though you've been working on it for two years. Don't be afraid to change the protagonist or the ending, or to decide that you are not writing about the theme you originally had in mind, but about something entirely different. That's O.K.

Record your voice as you read a chapter aloud, and be the objective listener this time as you play it back.

Type up two versions of a particular scene and compare them as if you were a disinterested observer.

Teach yourself organization. If you are serious about your writing, give it top priority in your schedule. No excuses. If morning is your best time to write, then schedule other demands on your time for the afternoon. If you work full time at another job, then set aside writing time on a regular basis whenever it works best for you—early morning, evenings, or weekends. There are, admittedly, exceptions to keeping a schedule. A brain tumor is an exception. Going to jail is an exception. But 99% of the things that we let interfere with our writing could be handled just as well at some other time of day. Too often we fool ourselves into believing that if we are doing something related to books—looking over new word processors, for example—we are writing. We are not writing.

And finally, when you are published, you can teach yourself professionalism in dealings with your editor. This means meeting deadlines, preferably not down to the wire. It means that you don't have to be goaded and coaxed and prodded by your editor to finish a book. What you may lack in talent you can sometimes make up in dependability. If editors have to choose between two equally fine manuscripts, they will choose the author who is more dependable and cooperative—and not temperamental. Finally, try to look at all suggestions from your editor objectively instead of immediately thinking of all the reasons why your editor was wrong. Most of the time editors are right. Not always, but nearly.

Knowing ourselves

We can teach ourselves to search for universals in the human experience, looking first in ourselves. What problems are we having in our own lives? What is it we worry about? In what simple things do we find joy?

While all of us have wondered about life after death, for example, some people dwell on it more than others. A book about a character worrying over the hereafter may attract a few readers, though probably not many. If we narrow it

down, however—condense it, distill it into a novel about a
widow who wishes that she had shown her husband more
appreciation in his lifetime, and that there was a way even
now that she could communicate all that had gone unsaid—
that touches the reader. We would all like another chance.

Conversely, a story about a man who allows no pets in his
home seems hardly to have enough depth for a novel. But if
we expand on this, making it only one characteristic of a
person who keeps everybody at arm's length, who is not
one for touching, who never lets his wife or children intrude
in his space, then readers are faced with a universal human
problem: How much of ourselves will we give, how much
time and caring will we have to spare and still leave some
for ourselves? Readers may not see themselves in a man
who allows no pets, but something about his problem
speaks to them all.

Sometimes we need to think small—to pinpoint what it is
we are worrying about so we can write about it effectively.
Other times we need to think big—to take an incident, a
personality, a conflict—and see it in a larger framework.

Most difficult in the area of self-teaching is getting in
touch with our own feelings. To know ourselves. There is
much about us we do not want to face. Yet, even if that is
especially true for certain writers, they can be true to
themselves by writing about *that* characteristic: a man or
woman who has trouble facing up to self-truths.

We don't have to be psychoanalyzed to write about the
human condition. But we must be aware of our limitations.
We must write about them, our failures as well as our
successes. We must be able to distinguish between righteous indignation and jealousy, between love and pos-
sessiveness, between humility and lack of self-esteem. Because in writing about other people, we are writing about

ourselves. In examining their strengths and weaknesses, we are probing our own. The best gift we can give ourselves is the determination to touch our deepest, most painful feelings, and the courage to write about them.

There will never be a time when we have "mastered" the art of writing. We will be learning and growing as writers for the rest of our lives. We will learn from teachers, workshops, editors, books—from everyday experiences—but mostly we will learn from the very act of putting words on paper.

Phyllis Reynolds Naylor

PHYLLIS REYNOLDS NAYLOR is the author of over 60 books, most of them novels, for both children and adults. A psychology major in college with plans to become a clinician, she helped pay her tuition by writing and selling short stories. After earning her B. A. degree, she decided that fiction was her first love and gave up plans for graduate school. She has been writing full time since 1960.

Some of her best-known works are *Crazy Love: An Autobiographical Account of Marriage and Madness* (Morrow); *Revelations* (St. Martin's Press); and *Unexpected Pleasures* (Putnam). *A String of Chances* won the South Carolina Young Adult Book Award; *The Keeper* was selected by the American Library Association Young Adult Services Division as a Best Book for Young Adults; and *The Year of the Gopher* was named Best Young Adult Book of the Year by the Young Adult Caucus of the Michigan Library Association. These and *Alice in Rapture, Sort Of* were all published by Atheneum.

Other books have earned her the Golden Kite Award from the Society of Children's Book Writers, the Child Study Award from Bank Street College, and the Edgar Allan Poe Award from Mystery Writers of America, as well as a number of American Library Association Notable citations. In 1987, Mrs. Naylor received a grant from the National Endowment for the Arts.

She and her husband live in Bethesda, Maryland, and are the parents of two grown sons.